TARPLEYWICK
A Century of Iowa Farming

TARPLEYWICK

A Century of Iowa Farming

HENRY C. TAYLOR

The Iowa State University Press, Ames

Composed and printed by The Iowa State University Press

First edition, 1970

International Standard Book Number: 0-8138-1690-4

Library of Congress Catalog Card Number: 70-103840

CONTENTS

PREFACE, vii

FOREWORD, ix

One   BEGINNINGS, 3

Two   EXPANSION, 18

Three   WOODS AND FIELDS, 23

Four   BUILDINGS AND FENCES, 27

Five   ACTIVITIES IN THE WOODYARD, 36

Six   ORCHARDS AND GARDENS, 44

Seven   LAND USE AND CROP ROTATION, 48

Eight   SEEDING AND CULTIVATION, 53

Nine   HARVEST, 62

Ten   LIVESTOCK, 72

Eleven   THE MARKETS, 76

Twelve   "IN-SERVICE TRAINING," 80

Thirteen   TARPLEY EARLY TAYLOR, 90

Fourteen   ELMIRA MARTIN TAYLOR, 101

Fifteen   THE RUBYS ❖ 1901–1916, 107

Sixteen   THE WILLE FAMILY ❖ 1917–1928, 113

Seventeen   TARPLEYWICK IN DISTRESS ❖ 1928–1944, 118

Eighteen   THE WARNERS, 121

INDEX, 131

Charles Henry Taylor as a 20-year-old Drake University student. This was in the summer of 1893, shortly before he decided to transfer to Iowa Agricultural College (now Iowa State University) and begin the formal study of agriculture. This youthful decision was to influence his life work, and the course of world agricultural economics.

Dr. Taylor at the height of his career as an internationally recognized agricultural economist.

PREFACE

I<small>N</small> A<small>PRIL</small>, 1966, I celebrated my ninety-third birthday and recalled that in April, 1896, the last semester of my senior year at Iowa State College, Ames, Iowa, I had returned to my father's farm to do the spring planting. This had been possible because, having finished all the work for the semester and having passed special examinations, I had fulfilled all the requirements for graduation by the tenth of April. For many years the reunions of the class of 1896 had been drawing me back to Ames to renew contact with my alma mater. Since the seventieth reunion was to be held in June, 1966, I decided not only to attend the alumni dinner but also to make a pilgrimage to the farm in southeastern Iowa where I had been born and had served my apprenticeship in farming. This book is an outgrowth of that pilgrimage.

The farm is located in Cedar Township, Van Buren County, Iowa, and although I did my last farming there in 1896, it remained in the family until 1916. In this book it is called Tarpleywick in honor of my father, Tarpley Early Taylor, and the ancestor for whom he was named.

The story of Tarpleywick begins at the time of the early settlement of Iowa and carries through to the present time. It tells how Tarpley Early Taylor assembled a five-hundred-acre farm by putting together eight small self-sufficing farms between 1860 and 1880. It tells of the changes which took place in methods of farming and the availability of markets. The railways came through and tapped this area for food for the growing cities; as a result, farming became increasingly commercial. As this happened the prices of the things the farmers sold compared to those of the things they bought became more and more important. The relative fluctuations in these prices spelled prosperity or depression. Consideration is given also to the changes in the ideas, skills, and outlook of those who farm the land. All these matters are portrayed in the swath of agricultural history presented in this volume.

The changes in farming recorded here took place against the background of national events and development. The following historical items need to be kept in mind: the Civil War, 1861–1865; the Homestead Act, 1862; the growth of land-grant colleges resulting from the land-grant acts (Morrill Acts) of 1862 and 1890; the depressions of 1873 and 1893, which had little effect on the farmers; World War I, 1914–1919; the agricultural depression of 1921; the general depression of 1929–1932; government regulation of agriculture, beginning in 1933 with price supports and production regulation; World War II, 1939–1946; and the continuation of government regulation of agriculture.

No one person could write the history of agriculture in the United States. It is not certain that one person could write the agricultural history of Iowa. But a wonderful result could be obtained if many people were to become interested in writing the history of individual farms. If they each were to write the history of one farm, the resulting collection of information would ultimately provide the basis for a specific and comprehensive picture of the dynamic factors with which farmers have to deal in order to be effective units in the national economy.

HENRY C. TAYLOR

FOREWORD

N O ONE is better qualified to write perceptively about a century of farming in Iowa than Henry C. Taylor. Born in Iowa in 1873, he was 96 years old when he died in May 1969. His lifetime spanned almost an entire century. An agricultural economist with a broad training in agriculture, he devoted several decades to the development of the discipline of agricultural economics and its influence on education, research, and public administration. He maintained a keen interest in worldwide agricultural affairs to the end of his life.

Dr. Taylor was the first professor of agricultural economics in a land grant institution, the author of the first American textbook dealing with the principles of agricultural economics, and the organizer and first Chief of the Bureau of Agricultural Economics in the U.S. Department of Agriculture. Following an assignment as the United States member of the permanent committee of the International Institute of Agriculture in Rome, Italy, he became the first Managing Director of the Farm Foundation in 1935. He retired in 1945 but continued as Agricultural Economist with the Foundation until 1949.

He received his undergraduate training at Drake University and Iowa State University. After earning his Master's degree at Iowa State, he studied at the London School of Economics and also spent one semester each at Halle Wittenberg University and the University of Berlin. He received his Ph.D. degree from the University of Wisconsin, where he later was head of the Department of Agricultural Economics for eleven years.

A scholar, Dr. Taylor was not only constantly seeking knowledge but was eager to share his discoveries with others who could benefit from the knowledge. His quest for knowledge took him to England, Germany, Italy, France, the Scandinavian countries, and also Japan, where he made agricultural tours. He stressed visits with farmers because he felt that those most directly involved could provide him with insights into a country's agriculture. He was often stimulated to start new projects by what he saw and learned.

When in 1957 the American Farm Economic Association instituted a program of electing outstanding agricultural economists as Fellows, Dr. Taylor was selected as one of the first recipients of the award. Prior to that he had been awarded an honorary LL.D. by the University of Wisconsin, an honorary Doctor of Political Science by the University of Freiberg, and a Distinguished Service Award by Drake University.

Best known perhaps among his many writings are his classic textbook, *Introduction to Agricultural Economics,* published in 1904, another early book, *Outline of Agricultural Economics,* and two comprehensive works which he co-authored in more recent years, *World Trade in Agricultural Products* and *The Story of Agricultural Economics.*

JOSEPH ACKERMAN
Managing Director, Farm Foundation

TARPLEYWICK
A Century of Iowa Farming

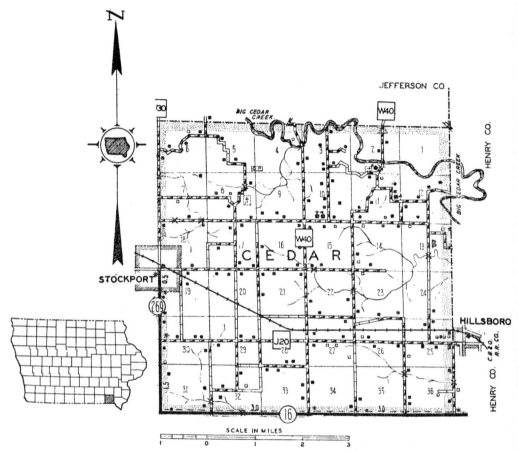

Cedar is the most northeastern township in Van Buren County. Tarpleywick was in sections 15 and 16. The small map locates Van Buren county in the state of Iowa.

Chapter 1

BEGINNINGS

THE FIRST TARPLEY in America, William, bought land in York County, Virginia, in 1635. In an old deed made by an officer of Lord Fairfax, the name Tarpley is spelled *Topley,* but there is no doubt concerning the correct spelling of the name because it appears in wills and other records from 1635 to the present day. As a rule, however, it is pronounced *Tapley.*

The first Taylor of our line, Richard, bought land in North Farnum Parish, Richmond County, Virginia, in 1664. Something more than seventy years later, toward the end of the 1730s, Richard's grandson, George Taylor, and William Tarpley's great-great-granddaughter, Mary Tarpley, were married in North Farnum Parish. This joined a member of the third generation of Taylors in America with a member of the fifth generation of Tarpleys in America and founded our branch of the family. Their second son, born in 1742, was the first Tarpley Taylor. He was my great-great-grandfather; my father, Tarpley Early Taylor, born in 1837, was named for him.

All my father's ancestors were pioneer farmers. On their way from Virginia to Iowa, they farmed in Hampshire County, West Virginia, and in Fleming County, Kentucky. My grandfather, William Early Taylor, brought his family to Cedar Township, Van Buren County, Iowa, in 1839.

When the territorial government of Iowa was organized in 1838, the land of southeastern Iowa had already been surveyed by the United States Government and put on sale. The townships had been divided into sections one mile

3

square, and beginning at the northeast corner of each township, these sections were numbered from 1 to 6 to the west and from 7 to 12 to the east, and so on. In Cedar Township, because of Big Cedar Creek, the first through road from east to west was two miles south of the north line of the township. When my immediate ancestors came to Iowa they settled land along this road, and it became the axis of a community made up of their friends and relatives.

The United States Census of 1840 shows the population of Iowa to have been about 45,000, most of which was located in the southeast corner of the state. A few of these settlers were in Cedar Township, but most of the land in the township was still unoccupied and much of it was held by speculators. Between 1840 and 1860 the population of the state grew to approximately 500,000, and the southeastern corner was one of the more favored areas.

When Grandfather Taylor and his family arrived in Cedar Township in 1839 they made their first home in a log cabin by the side of the east-west road mentioned above. Sometime during the ensuing year he purchased eighty acres of land in section 11, a mile and a half west of the cabin, but he did not build there until later. Not far from the north end of this eighty there was a large log house occupied by the Standley family. They proved to be the best neighbors anyone could wish for.

On July 22, 1840, about a year after the arrival of the Taylor family in Iowa, my grandmother, Mary Zumwalt Taylor, died of typhoid fever, leaving four little boys, the youngest a year old and the oldest nine. Warmhearted, capable Mrs. Standley took this motherless family into her home. As soon as my grandfather was sure that the children would be well cared for, he made a trip on horseback to his father's home in Flemingsburg, Kentucky.

Before coming to Iowa, William Early Taylor had run a blacksmith shop along with his farming. When he returned to Cedar Township after his visit in Kentucky, he built a blacksmith shop on the north end of his eighty, not far from the Standley home. His account book shows that he continued to ply his trade as an adjunct to his farming through 1845. After 1845 he devoted himself entirely to farming.

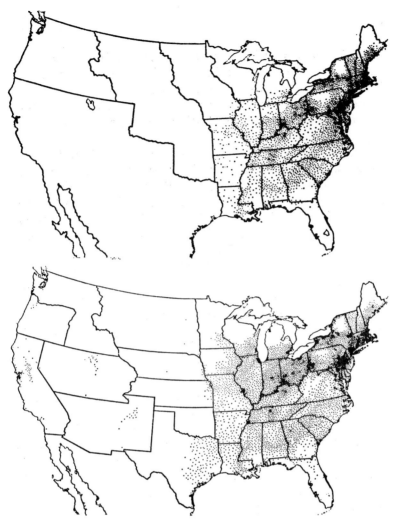

The rapid settlement of southeastern Iowa between 1840 and 1860 is readily apparent in the above maps, which show population in the United States in 1840 (above) and 1860 (below). Each dot represents 5,000 free citizens.

For more than a year after my grandfather built the blacksmith shop he and the little boys continued to live with the Standleys. However, one morning in November, 1841, he bridled a horse, threw a sack over its back, and rode north across Big Cedar Creek to the home of the Walker family. He did not tie up his horse and go into the house—he held his horse by the reins and asked to see Eliza, the twenty-eight-year-old unmarried daughter. When she came out, he asked her to marry him and she accepted. They had been acquainted for some time but there had been no courtship. On the twenty-third of November they married and set up housekeeping in the blacksmith shop, which had been converted into a home by the addition of a large fireplace at one end.

This marriage was most successful. Besides being a good mother to the four little boys and making a comfortable home for my grandfather, Eliza added two daughters and a son to the family. My father loved his stepmother and his half-sisters and was especially fond of his half-brother, Charlie. My grandfather died the same year I was born, 1873, but Eliza lived until 1884. From time to time she came to visit at Tarpleywick and told fascinating stories. She would sit in a small rocking chair smoking her clay pipe, and then, taking her pipe in her hand, she would tell a story. I heard the story of her marriage directly from her. She always had a happy look on her face when she spoke of life in the blacksmith shop and would add, "Those were my happiest days!" She also told stories she had heard in years gone by, many of which were local versions of Bible stories. I remember especially how interesting she made the story of the building of the Tower of Babel.

After my grandfather had become well acquainted with the character, topography, and native vegetation of the land, he bought 120 acres of prairie in sections 15 and 16,[1] a little over a mile west of his eighty. He plowed the prairie sod using two yokes of sturdy oxen hitched tandem to a sod-breaker plow. This plow had a sixteen-inch share made of steel which could be removed for sharpening and a wooden mouldboard designed to turn the furrow-slice over with the sod side down without breaking the slice. Corn could be planted in each third furrow-slice, and a good crop would grow with little further attention. The following year a crop of wheat could be grown on this land.

The family continued to live on the eighty while my grandfather broke the prairie, but he was planning to build a house and barns on the new farm. In order to have building material, he bought forty acres of timberland along Big Cedar Creek; and it was from this land that he took white

---

1. The NW$\frac{1}{4}$ of the NW$\frac{1}{4}$ of section 15 and the east $\frac{1}{2}$ of the NE$\frac{1}{4}$ of section 16 of Cedar Township.

oak logs to the local sawmill to be sawed into timbers and half-inch weatherboarding. Only when the farm work was not pressing was there time to cut logs and take them to the mill, so it took several years to cut and cure enough lumber. When, at last, the house was built, it was located on the northwest corner of section 15, that is to say, on the south side of the east-west road. It was a frame house with several rooms, each of which had a fireplace. Since the weatherboarding was rough-sawed, it was left unpainted. The family moved into this new home in 1847 when my father was ten years old.

The fireplaces mentioned above were the only means of heating the house, and all the cooking was done in the kitchen fireplace. Great quantities of firewood were needed for these fireplaces, and the same timberland that had furnished the lumber for the house now furnished fuel for heating and cooking. Just cutting and hauling this firewood was a big job!

The character of the farming done by William Early Taylor is recorded in the United States Census Schedules for his farm. The following is the Schedule for 1850:

Improved acres of land	120
Unimproved acres of land	40
Cash value of farm	$1,200
Value of farm implements and machinery	$ 100

Livestock, June 1, 1850:

Horses	2
Mules	2
Milch cows	4
Working oxen	4
Other cattle	1
Sheep	24
Swine	12

Value of livestock	$ 232

Produced during the year ending June 1, 1850:

Wheat, bushels	700
Indian corn, bushels	500
Oats, bushels	200
Wool, pounds	87
Butter, pounds	150
Hay, tons	2
Grass seeds, bushels	$3/4$
Value of homemade manufacturers	$ 73
Value of animals slaughtered	$ 122

Elmira and Tarpley Taylor had been married 13 years when this family photograph was made in 1874. Henry is on his father's knee. The older children are (left to right) Laura, Sylvanus, and Louelle.

It is apparent that the eighty acres in section 11 had been sold before 1850.

According to the Census Schedule of 1860, the value of the farm had increased. The acreage of improved land remained the same, but sixty-one acres of timberland had been added. I remember asking my uncle, Charlie Taylor, why Grandfather had not taken advantage of low land values to acquire more land. He told me that since there was unoccupied land which could be used at no cost for grazing and for cutting hay, there was no advantage to buying more land since taxes would have to be paid on purchased land. The Schedule of 1860 also showed that wheat production had declined and Indian corn had more than tripled; hay production had increased from two tons to sixteen tons; work oxen had disappeared; horses had increased from two to eleven and mules from two to four. The number of sheep had dropped from twenty-four to nine and wool from eighty-seven pounds to thirty-five pounds. This is associated with a decline in home manufactures from $73 to $50. In those days there were two reasons for keeping a few sheep, to have lamb or mutton for the table and to have wool for spinning. The spinning wheel and the loom were very important household equipment from 1840 to 1860. It is interesting to note that the value of animals slaughtered had been $122 in 1850 and had increased to $334 in 1860. The presence of two yokes of oxen in 1850 and their absence in 1860 indicates that all the prairie land in sections 15 and 16 had been broken before 1860. Although the records of the farming done by my grandfather are not plentiful, the achievements of my father at Tarpleywick indicate clearly that as a boy he had received excellent training in the art of farming.

Three other families, the Morrises, the Harlans, and the Martins, need to be introduced before we go on to the story of Tarpleywick. All three settled land along the east-west road in Cedar Township, and all three became important in our community.

Henry and Jane Morris came to Cedar Township from Harlan County, Kentucky, in 1838, the year before Grandfather Taylor and his family arrived. The Morrises moved from Kentucky by covered wagon, but instead of riding in the wagon as did most womenfolk, Jane Mark Morris rode horseback (sidesaddle) and carried her one-year-old son, Henry T., in her arms. This family became prominent in the community and later became related by marriage to the Taylors.

Much more important, however, was the migration of the Harlans and the Martins to Cedar Township in 1852, because it marked the arrival of my mother's family. Alexander Martin married Anna Harlan in 1833. Their fifth child, Elmira, who was to be my mother, was born February 14, 1843, in Union County, Indiana. The Harlans were quite a clan, and when my great-grandfather and great-grandmother Harlan came to Iowa they brought with them not only the Martins but also their other children, most of whom were married and had families of their own.

Both the Martins and the Harlans were Scotch-Irish from the north of Ireland. The Martins had gone to Ireland from Scotland, but the patriarch of the Harlan family, George Harland, went to Ireland from County Durham, England. He dropped the *d* from his name and established the Harlan family. His descendants in America run into the thousands.

In the spring of 1855, the people living along the east-west road became a united community with a goal; they wanted a school. They formed School District Number 2 and made plans to build a school. One of the leaders in this undertaking was Grandfather Taylor; the location chosen for the schoolhouse was a quarter mile east of his home. The acre of land for the schoolhouse cost only $10, but when the necessary materials had been assembled and paid for, the district treasury contained just $200. No one would build the schoolhouse for $200! The project seemed doomed to failure, but my grandfather came to the rescue and offered to build the school for that sum. The school opened as planned.

The one-room school building could accommodate forty children. The seats and desks, made of black walnut lumber by local carpenters, were wide enough for two people. They varied in height so that in the back of the room they were big enough for adults and in front they were small enough for five-year-olds. They were lined up in four rows lengthwise of the room, but the two inner rows were interrupted in the middle to make space for a large coal stove. In the front of the room, on a platform six inches above the floor, was the teacher's desk and on the wall behind it was a blackboard that extended the width of the room. In the early years, there were three terms of school. The spring and fall terms ran for two months, the winter term for four months. It was usual for a young woman to teach the fall and spring terms, but a man was preferred for the winter term when the older boys went to school. This school, unlike the traditional "little red schoolhouse," was painted white. Later it became known as the Taylor School and continued to be a center of community activity for over a century.

My father was eighteen years old when the schoolhouse was built; nevertheless for the next three years he attended school during the winter term. My grandfather had received elementary school education in Kentucky and is said to have gone to Virginia for some schooling when he was in his teens. His blacksmith account book shows that he wrote a good hand. It is probable, therefore, that my father had some instruction in reading, writing, and cyphering at home before he went to school. In any case, by the time he was twenty-one he had a good knowledge of reading, writing, and arithmetic, and I remember hearing him speak appreciatively of the man who taught school.

Elmira Martin was one of the first pupils to be enrolled in the new school. She made good use of her opportunity, because in later years she read and wrote with great facility. Whether she and Tarpley became acquainted at school or whether they had already met, we do not know, but they were in school together during the three winters that Tarpley attended school.

The introductions have all been made and the time has come to begin the story of Tarpleywick.

When Tarpley Early Taylor came of age on August 2, 1858, his father gave him a horse, a saddle, and bridle, and wished him well. He was free to leave home and begin a life of his own. His first independent move was to go on horseback to Louisiana, Missouri, to visit his maternal grandparents, the Zumwalts. He stayed with them for some time, probably through the winter, and did such work for wages as he could find. It is certain that he spent part of the time helping build the turnpike leading into the town of Louisiana.[2] We do not know what he did from the spring of 1859 to the spring of 1860 except that he had been earning money and saving it. We do know that he had returned to Van Buren County by July 24, 1860, because on that date he paid $800 for sixty acres[3] of land a mile south of his father's house. The sixty acres consisted of forty acres on the east side of the north-south road and twenty acres on the west side, both of which cornered on the center of Cedar Township. This was the beginning of Tarpleywick.

2. See Chapter 12, page 87.
3. The $W\frac{1}{2}$ of the $W\frac{1}{2}$ of the $SW\frac{1}{4}$ of section 15, and the $E\frac{1}{2}$ of the $SE\frac{1}{4}$ of the $SE\frac{1}{4}$ of section 16.

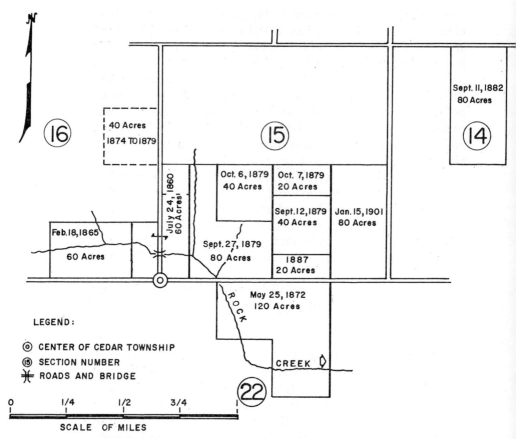

*How Tarpleywick grew. To the original home farm of 60 acres, Tarpley
Taylor had added an additional 540 acres by 1901.*

Tarpley put out his first crop in the spring of 1861.
There was a one-room log house at the southwest corner
of the forty, but he probably boarded at home with his
mother and father. However, we know that he was looking
forward to having a home of his own, because early that
spring Elmira Martin wrote a letter to her brother George,
who had enlisted in the army, telling him enthusiastically
of her engagement to Tarpley.

Tarpley and Elmira were married on the last day of
October and began housekeeping in the one-room log house.
Having received excellent training from her mother, Elmira
was skilled in all the household arts, including spinning and

weaving, and in the outdoor tasks considered in those days to be women's work: gardening and poultry raising. Besides learning how to grow the usual flowers, fruits, and vegetables, she had also learned to cultivate and use the plants important to the folk medicine of the time. Furthermore she knew the medicinal value of the various wild plants that grew in the area—a knowledge that was essential in those days when there was no doctor for miles around.

This was before the horse and buggy days. It might better be called the *horse and saddle* days. This explains why Tarpley bought a sidesaddle for Elmira so that she could have an easy means of going back and forth between Tarpleywick and the homes of her kinfolk.

Housekeeping was simple in the log cabin and the furnishings were limited. My mother used to tell of her first guest for a meal. Tarpley asked his half brother Charlie to have dinner with them. This must have been during the summer following their marriage because it was gooseberry time, and my mother picked some wild gooseberries for this occasion. Since her supply of dishes was very limited she heaped all the berries onto a large saucer. At dinner, when time came for dessert, she passed this dish to Charlie expecting him to take some of them on his plate and pass them on to Tarpley. Charlie, thinking it was a dish for him, set it down by his plate and ate all the berries. We must hasten to add that Charlie was only eleven years old at that time and that my mother always laughed when she told this story. She thought the joke was on her.

It is probable that Elmira did some spinning that first winter in the log cabin. Although there was no room for a loom, she undoubtedly had a spinning wheel. The wool was taken to Meek Brothers Woolen Mill in Bonapart to be carded. She may have done some weaving that winter on the loom at her father's home or the one at her father-in-law's home, which was only a mile away. It is certain that she spun wool into yarn and did a great deal of knitting. For many years she continued to practice the arts of spinning and weaving.

The young couple planted an orchard at once. They selected apple, plum, and peach trees, and many varieties of small fruit. When spring came they planted a garden. Most of their food came from the farm, and the garden was sup-

plemented by wild fruits—plums, gooseberries, and blackber-
ries—all of which were plentiful. In the early years some
wheat was always grown to provide flour for bread. Cornmeal
was also used of course. Bees were kept and sorghum was
grown; molasses was made at the local sorghum mill. Honey
or sorghum were used on the table to reserve the sugar for
canning or preserving fruits. Besides these products which
came directly from the land, they had butter, milk, eggs,
chickens, pork, beef, and lamb from their own production.

Elmira traded butter and eggs at the country store for
the few articles they had occasion to buy. Tarpley never
used tobacco or liquor of any kind. Neither Tarpley nor
Elmira drank coffee or tea. Salt and sugar, calico and thread,
and miscellaneous small items made up their purchases.
Thus the farm economy was so nearly self-sufficing that most
of the money received from the sale of grain, grass seed, and
livestock was available for buying more land and for building a frame house, a barn, and other buildings.

In the spring of 1862 Tarpley prepared the land, sowed
wheat broadcast, and harrowed it in. Then came the preparation for the planting of corn. Having plowed the ground
with a twelve-inch walking plow of the mouldboard type
drawn by two horses and having put the soil in readiness
for planting, he asked Elmira to help him plant the field.
Mother used to tell about this saying, "Tarpley made a
furrow with a single-shovel plow drawn by one horse. I followed with a bag of seed corn and dropped two grains of seed
each step forward." When Tarpley had made one round,
he used the same equipment to cover the seed by running
a light furrow alongside the one in which the seed had been
dropped. Thus Tarpley made two rounds with his single-
shovel plow while Elmira made one round dropping the
seed.

When the corn was large enough to be cultivated, the
same single-shovel plow was used for running a furrow on
each side of each row of corn and for breaking out the middle
by running a furrow halfway between the rows. Since the
corn could not be cultivated across the rows and herbicides
had not been dreamed of, some hoeing and pulling of weeds
was necessary to produce a good crop.

Elmira did not do any hoeing of corn at Tarpleywick.
However, I heard her tell of hoeing corn for her father when

*The fields of Tarpleywick were first plowed
in 1862 with a mouldboard plow.*

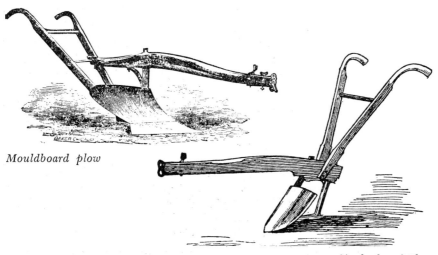

Mouldboard plow

Single-shovel plow

she was sixteen years old. Her father hired a woman to work
with her in hoeing ten acres of corn. She said, "That was
the first time I knew what it was to be tired." She was none-
theless very busy that first summer at Tarpleywick. Besides
her usual chores, there were fruits and vegetables to be
canned, dried, or preserved for winter use, and most important her first child—my older brother, Sylvanus—was born
August 8.

At harvest time Tarpley cut the wheat with a cradle,
mowed his hay crop with a scythe, and picked the corn by
hand using a wooden husking peg. An itinerant threshing
machine was available for threshing wheat and oats.

After the birth of Sylvanus, Father and Mother began
to plan to build a house.[4] As his father had done before
him, Tarpley bought timberland along Big Cedar Creek in
order to have building material, but unlike his father he
was able to obtain pine lumber for the exterior of the house.
The twenty acres[5] of timberland he got was two and a quarter miles north of Tarpleywick but only about a mile and a
half from Meshak Sigler's water power grist and sawmill.
This mill was not built until 1853, so it was not the one
used by my grandfather. Whenever the work on the farm
permitted, Father cut and hauled white oak logs to the
sawmill. Then the lumber had to be hauled from the sawmill and carefully stacked so that it would cure properly.
This oak material provided the sills, the studding, the plates,
the joists, the rafters, and the floors of the four-room, story-
and-a-half frame house that was finished early in 1866. The
exterior was of pine lumber and this had to be hauled by
team and wagon from Fort Madison on the Mississippi. It
was sawed from logs that had been floated in rafts down the
Wisconsin and Mississippi Rivers from the great pine forests
of Wisconsin. Fort Madison had sawmills and planing mills
where doors and windows, weatherboarding, and shingles
could be bought.

---

4. I had always known that the exterior of the house was of pine lumber
drawn from Fort Madison. I had no definite information about the other
materials beyond what I had seen as a boy, the oak floors and the oak joists
under the floors that could be seen in the cellar. However, when I visited
the present owner of Tarpleywick, C. A. Warner, he told me that he had
torn down the old house and said that the entire frame as well as the floors
had been built of oak. This information enabled me to trace the source of
all the materials for the house.
5. The W$\frac{1}{2}$ of the NW$\frac{1}{4}$ of the SW$\frac{1}{4}$ of section 3 of Cedar Township.

It took two days for Father to drive a team hitched to a wagon the 35 miles to Fort Madison and back with a load of lumber. In one day he could get to Fort Madison and load the lumber. The following day, by an early start, he could return to Tarpleywick before dark. In order that these trips would not interfere with the work on the farm, he did this hauling in the wintertime.

Elmira and Tarpley began to plan their new home in 1862, soon after the birth of Sylvanus, and it was shortly after the birth of their second child, Laura, on May 24, 1866, that they moved in. The year before the house was finished, Father had enlarged Tarpleywick by an additional sixty acres of land in section 16.[6] This gave him a total of eighty acres across the road to the west of the house. Certainly the young family was prospering.

6. The court records show that on February 18, 1865, Tarpley Taylor acquired the W¾ of the S½ of the SE¼ of section 16.

Cradling wheat at Tarpleywick
in the early days

Cradle scythe

EXPANSION

THE EXPANSION of Tarpleywick actually began in 1865 (as we have seen in the preceding chapter), and it continued over the next twenty years. The Civil War had just ended at the beginning of this growth, and the Homestead Act continued to attract farmers to seek larger farms in the West during this entire twenty-year period.

Up to 1870, facts regarding Tarpley's farming are scarce, but fortunately his United States Census Schedule for that year is available.

His Schedule, dated July 26, 1870, contains the following information:

Improved acres of land		110
Unimproved acres of land		20
Cash value of farm		$3,900.00
Value of farm implements and machinery		$ 250.00
Total amount of wages paid during the year		$ 56.00
Livestock as of June 1, 1870:		
	Horses	2
	Milk Cows	2
	Swine	20
	Mules and asses	5
	Sheep	12
Value of livestock		$ 757.00
Produced during the year ending June 1, 1870:		
	Wheat, bushels	95
	Indian corn, bushels	1,260
	Oats, bushels	105
	Wool, pounds	59
	Potatoes Irish	40
	(bushels) Sweet	10

Butter, pounds	200
Hay, tons	8
Seed, grass, bushels	20

Value of animals slaughtered or sold for slaughter:

$ 438.00

Estimated value of all farm production, including
betterments and additions to stock $1,117.11

In speaking of the acreage of Tarpleywick, the timber-land in section 3 is never included because he had sold his brother William the 10 acres at the north end of the forty, east of the road. This explains why there are only 110 acres of improved land on the schedule.

On May 25, 1872, Tarpley added 120 acres to his farm. This land was in section 22, which lies across the road south of section 15. This purchase included the west half of the NE¼ of section 22 and the NE¼ of the NW¼ of section 22. The 120 acres cost $1,440. About half this land was good crop land and the remainder was pasture land. The part of the pasture that lay along Rock Creek had a great many trees on it, and where there were no trees, there was a good deal of hazel brush.

William Early Taylor, Tarpley's father, died December 12, 1873. In the settlement of the estate in 1874, Tarpley acquired 40 acres of land consisting of the SE¼ of the NE¼ of section 16.

At the beginning of the year 1879, Tarpleywick consisted of 270 acres, but before the end of that year it had been expanded to 410 acres. Tarpley had purchased the remaining 80 acres in the SW¼ of section 15 (except the 10 acres in the NW corner, which he had sold to his brother William) and the west half of the SE¼ of section 15 with the exception of the south 20 acres. Besides expanding his holdings, he also consolidated them. He traded the 40 acres in section 16, which he had inherited from his father in 1874, for 40 acres owned by Jabez Ruby in section 15. Both parties benefited by this trade because the 40 acres in section 16 lay adjacent to the homeland of Jabez Ruby and because Tarpley had acquired, or was in the process of acquiring, the land on three sides of the Ruby 40 in section 15.[1]

1. Detailed description of purchases: Sept. 12, 1879, the S½ of the NW¼ of the SE¼ of section 15 and the N½ of the SW¼ of the SE¼ of section 15; Sept. 27, 1879, the SE¼ of the SW¼ of section 15 and the E½ of the W½ of the SW¼ of section 15; Oct. 7, 1879, the N½ of the NW¼ of the SE¼ of section 15.

Thus for the farming year of 1879 Tarpley farmed 270 acres, but for the farming year 1880 he farmed 410 acres. This must have caused some problems in answering the questions for the 1880 census, because the acreage and livestock were to be given for 1880 but the crops were supposed to be given for 1879. On the basis of the facts I have which the Director of the Census for 1880, Francis A. Walker, did not have, I have edited the Schedule for 1880. Tarpley reported on the production of all the 410 acres which he possessed in 1880, even though someone else farmed 140 acres of this land in 1879. As edited, the Census Schedule for 1880 reads as follows:

1880—Cedar Township—Van Buren Co.—June 26, 1880

TARPLEY E. TAYLOR (owner)

Acres of land improved	410
Tilled acres	195
Meadows, permanent pastures, orchards, vineyards	215
Acres of woodland and forest unimproved	57
Farm implements and machinery	$227.00
Livestock	$1,238.00
Fences, cost of building and repairing in 1879	$10.00
Fertilizers, cost of that purchased in 1879	none

Labor:
Amount paid for wages in 1879	$73.00
Weeks of hired labor in 1879	
(exclusive of housework)	10
Estimated value of all farm productions	$1,396.00

Grassland:
Acreage mown in 1879	40
Hay harvested in 1879, acres	36
Grass seed harvested in 1879, acres	60

(The grass seed mentioned was timothy seed.)

Horses on hand, June 1, 1880	9

Cattle:
Milk cows on hand, June 1, 1880	8
Other	11
Calves dropped, 1879	7
Cattle purchased, 1879	4
Cattle sold, living, 1879	6
Cattle slaughtered, 1879	1
Cattle died, strayed, stolen, and not recovered	1

Butter made on farm, 1879, pounds		400
Sheep:		
On hand, June 1, 1880		34
Lambs dropped, 1879		11
Lambs slaughtered, 1879		1
Lambs killed by dogs, 1879		2
Clip, spring 1880, shorn and to be shorn		
(pounds)	Fleeces	23
	Weight	127
Swine on hand June 1, 1880		90
Poultry (barnyard) on hand June 1, 1880		
(exclusive of spring hatching)		90
Eggs produced in 1879, dozen		900

Produced during 1879:		
Indian Corn	acres	74
	bushels	2400
Wheat,	acres	10
	bushels	78
Oats,	acres	15
	bushels	545
Flax,	acres	12
	bushels	144
Sorghum,	acres	$\frac{1}{4}$
	molasses, gallons	26
Potatoes (Irish)	acres	$\frac{1}{4}$
	bushels	35
Apples,	acres	3
	bearing trees	100
	bushels	50

Total value of orchard products sold or consumed $25.00

Forest products, value of all forest
products sold or consumed in 1879 $40.00

At the time of the United States Census for 1880, Tarpleywick had been enlarged to 410 acres. It continued to grow. In 1882, when the Alexander Martin estate was settled, 80 acres of pasture land on which there was a coal bank was added,[2] and in 1887 the purchase from Elda Blundy of 20 acres in section 15[3] evened off the east edge of the farm. With these two additions Tarpleywick was expanded to 510 acres and remained this size until the end of the century. This is the area to be held in mind during the discussion of the farming at Tarpleywick as it was carried on by Tarpley Early Taylor from 1880 to 1900.

2. The E½ of the NW¼ of section 14.
3. The S½ of the SW¼ of the SE¼ of section 15.

How did Tarpleywick compare in size with the average farm in Van Buren County? The average size of farms in Van Buren County in 1880 was 128 acres, in 1890 it was 143 acres, and in 1900 it was 134 acres. Thus Tarpleywick was 3.9 times the average size in 1880, 3.5 times the average size in 1890, and 3.8 times the average size in 1900. Furthermore, it was a much larger farm than had ever been held by any of Tarpley's direct line of Taylor ancestors in America.

Chapter Three

WOODS AND FIELDS

ROCK CREEK flows across Tarpleywick in a southeasterly direction, traversing meadows and meandering through woodland pastures. This creek and the woodland along it are very important. As we have already noted, the main part of Tarpleywick had been native prairie, so there were no trees on it, but some of the land along Rock Creek was fringed with trees and hazel brush. This fringe broadened as the creek flowed across the farm. In section 15 varieties of oak, hickory, elm, aspen, thornbush, and plum grew on both sides of the creek. The same varieties grew abundantly in the wooded area in section 22, and in addition, there was hazel brush skirting the timber area along the creek. With the crooks and turns characteristic of all streams, Rock Creek creates a water hole here and there where cattle may drink, where little boys may go swimming, and where minnows, small fish, tadpoles, and turtles make their homes. When I was a boy these water holes provided the cattle in the pastures that bordered the creek with adequate drinking water most of the year. In dry years wells had to be depended upon to supplement the water holes in sections 15 and 16, but no wells were required for the pastures in section 22.

The area of trees and hazel brush along Rock Creek provided the boys of Tarpleywick and their neighbors with a hunting ground. One of my early memories is going rabbit hunting with my brother Sylvanus, who was eleven years older than I. A most interested member of our party was

Fido, a black and yellow mongrel, who stood only about a foot high. As my brother reached up to take down the shotgun from its rack, Fido jumped up and down and expressed his excitement in easily understood dog language. When we got into the hunting area, my brother and I stood on the field side of a rail fence that separated tillage land from an area where hazel brush covered the ground except for occasional open grass plots a few rods wide. Fido knew his part. He entered the hazel brush and we stood facing the area, watching. There was complete understanding between Fido and Sylvanus. Fido was silent until he stirred up a rabbit, then he gave his characteristic yelp, and drove the rabbit across the grass plot in front of which his master was standing. As the rabbit crossed the grass plot my brother performed his part in accordance with Fido's expectations. Then Fido picked up the rabbit, carried it to his master and laid it down at his feet. He then looked at my brother, who was by that time reloading his old muzzle-loading shotgun. Sylvanus waved his hand and Fido was off to find another rabbit. These were exciting occasions for a boy of six or seven years. Rabbit hunting in the hazel brush came to a close when my brother married in 1883 and moved to his own home. It was several years before I carried a gun. In the meantime Fido had gone to his reward, and Father had removed the hazel brush and converted this area into good bluegrass pasture.

The passing of the hazel brush created another loss. In the days when the hazel brush was thriving, a great abundance of hazel nuts were gathered each autumn. These nuts were dried out in the hulls and stored for winter use. Along with hickory nuts, walnuts, and butternuts, they added greatly to the satisfaction of the family in the winter months.

When I was about fourteen years old my father bought me a one-shot, 22-calibre Flobert rifle. My era of hunting fitted into the period when there was no dog at Tarpleywick. By that time, many Osage orange hedges grew on the farm and these provided nesting places for rabbits. My rabbit hunting consisted of walking along the field side of these hedges with my eyes searching for rabbits. Fortunately for my quest, when a rabbit was sighted it usually sat perfectly still long enough for the little rifle to perform its function, and a rabbit would hang by its hind legs from my belt.

My Flobert rifle also served well in squirrel hunting. The larger trees along Rock Creek afforded nesting places for squirrels. My eye soon became trained in spotting squirrels lying flat on their bellies on a horizontal limb of a large oak tree. In those days a nearly grown young squirrel was a delicacy and was often dressed and sent as a special token of friendship to some neighbor who was sick. I did not always hunt alone. Often on a Saturday afternoon, four or five of the neighbor boys would get together for a squirrel hunt—usually with more conversation and recreation than game-bagging.

Some of the abundant wildlife was predatory and some of it was beautiful and innocent, such as the rabbits and squirrels. The predatory animals—wolves, foxes, raccoons— did not particularly disturb life at Tarpleywick, but the skunk was a great nuisance. In their day, Sylvanus and Fido protected the chicken yard at Tarpleywick from the ravages of the skunk, a job I assumed after I received the Flobert rifle. I developed skill in finding the dens where skunks multiplied. A typical den was a hole near the foot of a big hollow oak tree. I would face this hole two or three feet away and pound on the ground. This would bring the skunk to investigate, and as it showed the white streak on the front of its face, a bullet ended its life. A comment by Frank Clark, who at the time was living in the tenant house at Rock Creek, indicates that my rifle and I proved effective: "Henry is better than any dog in protecting our chicken yards from the skunks."

Of the birds, the hawks and the crows were the predatory ones that had to be kept from the chicken yard. Both the shotgun for shooting them on the wing and the rifle for shooting them on the nest were used effectively. There were also many innocent and beautiful birds about the homestead and in the field. The house wren came year after year to the same nest under the eaves of the house. The robins, harbingers of spring, enjoyed the lawn and were much enjoyed by the family. On one occasion, in the early nineties, my sister Carrie was playing the piano near the open window. When she played "Robins in the Woodland" the robins in the yard joined their voices with the tones of the piano.

The hummingbirds and the wild canaries are well remembered. Other birds were the sparrows; some of them sang beautifully and were highly appreciated. Others, too numerous, were looked upon as a nuisance. Then there were the jays, which were good to look at, but whose voices were not pleasant. The woodpeckers and flickers were regarded as friends of the woodland.

The bird I enjoyed most in the field was the meadowlark sitting on the rail fence singing. As I cultivated corn, the blackbirds often followed in the row to pick up forms of life the shovel had turned up. The doves were often seen gleaning in the green fields after the wheat and oats had been cut. The boys with shotguns called them wild pidgeons and carried many of them home where they were used as a dainty on the table.

The fact that Rock Creek passed through Tarpleywick farm had a profound influence upon the type of farming used. The drainage of the main part of the farm is entirely taken care of by this creek and its tributaries. The fields slope gradually toward the stream and steep slopes are rare. As we have seen, the creek flows through the farm in a southeasterly direction, crossing the pasture land in section 16 and the woodland pastures in sections 15 and 22. In my father's day, the branches that enter Rock Creek were not bordered by trees (except for willows planted to reduce erosion), and cultivation was carried fairly close to the edge of these streams where they passed through tillage land.

All the land is well drained. For this reason good crops can be grown at Tarpleywick every year, whereas the crops on the gumbo land of the flat prairies around Stockport often fail because of lack of drainage. This good drainage at Tarpleywick does introduce the problem of knowing how to handle the land to keep erosion to a minimum. However, as long as Tarpleywick remained in the Taylor family this was never a problem.

Livestock, the one means of making use of pasture land, became the central feature of the farming done there, and it will be dealt with in a later chapter.

BUILDINGS AND FENCES

THE WHITE HOUSE at the center of Cedar Township, which Tarpley built for his family in 1866, was the focal point of the farm operation at Tarpleywick. Two tenant houses, each of which had a privy, a hen house, and a barn for a milk cow and horses, also stood on the farm. The first house near Rock Creek, a quarter mile east of the Tarpleywick residence, was used for a hired man— a cropper—who worked for Tarpley. The second, on the "coal bank eighty" in section 14, was occupied by a man who operated the coal bank. He dug the coal and sold it to schools, churches, stores and some homes in the surrounding area, and received a share of the proceeds. When the coal digging did not require his attention, he worked for Tarpley by the day.

Water was provided by dug wells accessible to the houses and the barns. Other wells were located in the pastures where cattle might require water when the creek was low in dry seasons. In 1890 a windmill was constructed at the well across the road from the farmhouse, and pipes carried the water to tanks for the cattle in the pastures in sections 16 and 15.

Water for my father's house was provided by a dug well on the west side of the house and by a cistern at the east door of the kitchen. For many years the water was drawn from the well by means of a windlass and an oaken bucket, but about 1890 this was replaced by a cast iron pump. The water from the cistern was drawn by means of

27

The house and horse barn at Tarpleywick. This photograph was made in the early 1900s when the farm was the home of the John W. Ruby family.

a chain pump. In Tarpley's day the house did not have running water.

The horse barn and other important sheds were built around a barnyard to the east of the farmhouse. Not far from the kitchen door was the dinner bell, mounted on a ten-foot oak post. This bell could be heard easily all over Tarpleywick.

The building nearest the house was a red smokehouse. It was sixteen feet long and twelve feet wide, and served also as the loom house and the carpenter shop. Smoking of meat took only a few weeks each winter. At this time a cast iron kettle, about two and one-half feet in diameter, stood in the middle of the floor to serve as a smoke pot, and the hams and sides of bacon were hung from the rafters. A workbench well equipped with tools stretched along the wall under the windows on the west side. My brother Sylvanus made himself a sleigh in this workshop. At the south end of the room was the large loom, which in the early days was so very important. I can remember that flannel was woven on this loom when I was a boy, but later on it was used only for weaving rag carpets. The garden tools were also kept in the smokehouse. The domestic economy of the woodyard will be described in a later chapter.

About a hundred feet from the north end of the farmhouse was the privy, which was painted bright yellow. And a short distance to the right of the privy was the hen house, which was painted red. East of the hen house about fifty feet stood the corncrib-wagon-shed which served as the "ever-normal" granary. It was painted red. To the east and somewhat north of this corncrib there was a series of pigpens and cattle sheds which formed the north side of what we called "the barn lot." This barn lot extended over to the east-west road. The horse barn, located in the center of the west side of the barn lot, was about 200 feet from the kitchen door and was painted red. The carriage house stood south of the horse barn just to the west of the barn lot, near the east-west road, and it was painted red.

The horse barn, built sometime in the 1860s, had standing room for sixteen horses. It had a limestone basement where there were eight double stalls, four on each side, with a feed room between. Above the basement were three fourteen-foot bents. The barn was built on slightly sloping ground with the west side of the basement built into the bank; thus it was easy to construct a ramp on that side so that a team and wagon could be driven into the center bent of the mow. This driveway greatly facilitated the unloading of hay and grain to be stored.

The bent on the left side of the driveway was used entirely for hay. The one on the right side was devoted to granaries for the first eighteen or twenty feet, and the remainder of the floor space in that bent was used for storing tools and machinery. Above the bins for grain and the space used for implements, additional hay was stored.

The "ever-normal" granary corncrib was built about the middle of the 1870s. A considerable share of the corn crop—that which was to be fed to hogs and cattle during the winter—was stored in temporary pens made of fence rails such as were used in making the "zigzag" fences so common in that day. But Tarpley had the idea of the "ever-normal" granary and wanted to carry over enough corn from a good crop year to supplement a poor crop in finishing his hogs. For this purpose he built a double corncrib. Each crib was

H. C. Taylor returned to Tarpleywick for a visit in June, 1966. Although the original farmhouse had been replaced, the horse barn looked much as he had remembered it from his boyhood. The broad ramp still leads to the central doors through which he had driven wagon-loads of hay and grain. The ever-normal granary is on Dr. Taylor's left.

about thirty feet long and seven feet wide; between them there was a driveway broad enough to shelter a farm wagon and yet leave room enough on each side of the wagon for a man to walk. One roof covered the two cribs and the driveway between them. The cribs were set on posts about two feet up from the ground with tin pans on the tops of the posts so that rats could not climb the posts and get into the granary. The outside of each crib was covered with vertical weatherboarding, but the side along the driveway was enclosed with three-inch wooden strips spaced about a quarter inch apart so that air could circulate between the strips and through the corn. This double crib was built about 1876 and is still in use today.

From the earliest days Tarpley had sheds for the cattle and sheep. These varied in form and degrees of permanence. The simplest shed was made by bringing some ten-foot posts from the woodlot and setting them in the ground about two feet. Poles were put across the top of these posts to serve as plates, and smaller poles were laid on the plates close enough together to support a roof of straw. This shed might be weatherboarded with locally sawed lumber and have only the top covered with straw, or the pole frame might be left open and "finished" at threshing time by building the straw pile around it so as to leave only the south side open.

In later years, Tarpley's cattle sheds were made entirely of lumber from the local sawmill. These sheds, also open on the south side, were not warm in winter, but they broke the wind, sheltered the livestock from snow and rain, and gave them a dry place to lie down. On a sunny day in wintertime these sheds were very comfortable, even though the day might be cold with a keen wind blowing from the northwest.

About 1877 Tarpley built a combination hay barn, corncrib, and sheep barn on the west eighty across the road from the house. This barn was weatherboarded with pine lumber, but the framework was made of hewed timbers. It had a large hayloft equipped with a track for a horse-drawn hay fork, and the hay was put into the barn from the south end through a large hay door. This barn proved to be exceedingly useful for storing hay and feeding livestock. Furthermore, the amount of hay stacked in the fields and fed on the ground was greatly reduced.

A somewhat similar hay barn was built near the tenant house a quarter mile east of the homestead, but not until 1894. With three good-sized barns, practically all of the hay was put under a roof. The livestock were better housed, and on cold winter days far more work was done in a sheltered place.

One shed with pens adjacent to it was used exclusively for hogs. Usually about fourteen brood sows were carried over the winter and needed to be sheltered during the coldest months so that the spring pigs would be born in comfortable farrowing pens. When spring came the sows and their litters of pigs were put into a small pasture next to the

The ever-normal granary. H. C. Taylor and Tarpleywick's present owner Gus Warner stand before the former driveway and wagon shelter; it has since been boarded up to serve as additional corn storage.

Fanning mill

feeding pens. In very bad, wet, cold, weather they could be put under shelter, but in the main they were raised in the open and had access both to troughs for slopping and to the feeding areas. There was no close confinement for the pigs as they were growing up. By late November, or earlier, all the spring pigs had gone to market and the herd of hogs had been reduced to the old sows and the gilts which were being kept for breeding purposes. A few litters of fall pigs might remain, but Tarpley gave special attention to the spring pig crop.

Certain equipment used in the barns and corncribs needs to be mentioned. The haymow in each of the three barns had a track and carrier for a horse-drawn hayfork. Of the other machines, the fanning mill was perhaps the most important. It stood in the horse barn near the granaries. Operated by manpower, it was used for cleaning the small grain and timothy and clover seed used for seeding purposes on the farm. A great variety of sieves could be used in turn according to the kind of seed to be cleaned. A hand crank turned a rotary fan which blew out all the lighter materials mixed with the seed and provided power for shaking the sieves so that heavier small particles would go through the sieves and be separated from the seeds. This machine did not always do a perfect job, but it greatly reduced the amount of weed seeds sown.

In the earlier days seed corn was shelled by hand, and the grains on the butts and tips of the ears were discarded so that the grains used for seed would be of uniform size.

Corn sheller

But in later years a corn sheller was used for shelling the seed corn after the grains unsuitable for seed had been removed. This machine was turned by hand and was also used for shelling corn for the chickens and lambs.

A horsepower mill for grinding corn on the cob for cattle feed was located outdoors just east of the "ever-normal" granary. This was a cast iron mill with a sheet iron hopper. The mill was fastened to a wooden box fourteen inches high, five feet long, and three feet wide, which was open at one end. The ears of corn were placed in the hopper and the ground corn and cobs dropped into the box below. Power was carried to this cast iron mill by placing two six-by-six-inch beams, one on each side of the upper burr. These beams were about twelve feet long and came together at the outer end. A team was hitched to the end of the beams and the horses walked in a circle around the mill turning the top burr against the bottom one. The corn could be put in the hopper while the mill was in action, but from time to time the horses had to be stopped long enough for the box containing the corn and cob meal to be emptied. A set screw at the top of the mill, extending up higher than the hopper, could be adjusted so that the burrs would grind the corn and cobs to the degree of fineness desired. This mill was used a great deal. I well recall that the operation of this corn mill frequently provided a job for me on Saturday when I was going to school in the winter.

There were three kinds of fences on Tarpleywick: split rail, Osage orange hedges, and wire. The split rail fences were of the zigzag stake and rider type. From a bird's-eye view, such a fence with its zigs and zags would occupy a strip about four feet wide. Each straight section, called a panel, was made of oak rails ten feet long. At the angles, the ends of the rails in one section overlapped the ends of the rails in the next one. In each panel the rails were laid one above the other to a height of about three and one-half feet. Each angle was buttressed by two stakes eight feet long, one on each side of the fence. These stakes had one sharp end which was placed in the ground. Then they crossed on top of the rails and rose above them, forming a long legged X, perpendicular to the line of the fence. A rail was then laid on with one end under the crossed stakes at one end of the panel and the other on top of the crossed stakes at the other end of the panel. Finally, a last rail was laid straight in the crotch of the stakes. These last two rails were the riders. The stakes held the lower part of the fence solid, and the riders held the stakes firm, besides giving added height to the fence. This type of fence would turn all kinds of live-stock if it had been well built; and if it were made of good oak material, it would last for many years with little care.

As a result of buying land, Tarpley had more rail fences than he needed because he did not want the small fields the former owners had chosen to have. Gradually the amount of rail fence decreased, but there was still a great deal on Tarpleywick in 1900. The old discarded rails were brought unforgettably to my attention because they were hauled to the woodyard and I sawed them up into stove lengths with a bucksaw.

The Osage orange hedge was planted by Tarpley in the 1870s. I am sure he planted more than a half mile. And he acquired that much again with the land he purchased in 1879. When the young trees were seven or eight feet high they were lopped, that is, bent in one direction until the stems angled about 35 degrees up from the ground. In order that they would not spring back up, they were hacked near the ground, perhaps a fourth or a third of the way through the stem. This would leave the hedge about four feet high and bring the stems of the hedge closer together and at an angle that would much better prevent the livestock from pushing their way through it. It would turn sheep and cattle, but it was not good for turning hogs. Furthermore, it had to be trimmed twice a year to keep it the right size. The aim was not to let it grow over four and one-half feet high and to keep its sides trimmed as well as its top. This trimming was done with a sharp corn knife, which would whip off the new growth of the hedge when it was still rela-tively soft. By cutting the hedge just after corn planting time and again after harvest, it could be kept the right size. But if it were left for a whole year, then the bushes became trees and chopping off the tops and burning them became a burdensome task.

By 1880 wire fence became available, both barbed wire and wire netting. Tarpley used both. All the fences built of new material after 1880 were wire fences. These were sometimes just three or four strands of barbed wire which would turn cattle. At other times a two-foot strip of wire netting was placed at the bottom and two strands of barbed wire were strung above that, spaced to make a four-foot fence. This would turn sheep, cattle, and hogs, and was a good kind of fence for Tarpleywick.

The outside fences, those along the road, and those separating Tarpleywick from the neighbors' land, were the important fences. As time went on Tarpley maintained fewer and fewer fences within the boundaries of the farm. In section 15 there was one field of 120 acres and another of more than 60 acres. In section 16 all the land west of the orchard was in one field with the exception of the pasture along Rock Creek and a 10-acre field north of Rock Creek, which was the favorite field for "hogging-down" corn and which was securely enclosed with hog-proof fence.

The buildings and fences were planned and built to complement the land utilization best suited to Tarpleywick. Chapter 7 enlarges upon this subject and tells of the field operations as they were carried out by my father.

ACTIVITIES IN THE WOODYARD

THE WOODYARD at Tarpleywick occupied an area north of the farmhouse. A paling fence ran east and west separating the house yard from the woodyard. This fence was about twenty feet north of the house and was made of locally sawed oak pickets about three inches wide. It ran from the northwest corner of the smokehouse to the white picket fence on the west side of the lawn. At the end of the fence by the corner of the smokehouse was a four-foot gate through which we passed from the house yard to the woodyard. The north side of the woodyard was bounded by the henhouse, the privy, and a fence made of six-inch boards. The west side of this yard was enclosed by an Osage orange hedge, a twelve-foot gate, and a panel of fence made of oak pickets. There was no fence on the east side, but the limit was set by the rat-proofed, "ever-normal" granary-corncrib. Although the chickens had free access to this whole area, they usually congregated on the north side of the woodyard in front of the hen house.

Fall, winter, and spring were the times of the year when the woodyard was a busy place with at least five different activities being carried on in the woodyard, all related to the self-sufficient economy of the household. They were: making apple butter, hog killing, preparation of the wood supply for heating and cooking, soapmaking, and beekeeping.

In apple harvest time, after the cider apples had been to the mill, a big copper kettle at least two and one-half feet across the top and more than two feet deep was placed on stones so that a fire could be built under it. It was then filled with apple cider, the fire was started, and the cider was gradually boiled down. At the same time, the womenfolk were all busy peeling and coring apples and cutting them into quarters. The quartered apples were added to the cider kettle while someone kept stirring the kettle—a joint process that took many hours. A paddle was used for stirring the apple butter. It was made of a three-quarter-inch board about two and one-half feet long and three or four inches wide, to which was attached at right angles a round handle about six feet long. After the apple butter began to thicken it had to be stirred constantly to keep it from sticking to the bottom of the kettle. This was my job when I was a boy. I had to keep the lower end of the stirring paddle continuously moving over the bottom of the kettle to make sure the thickening apple butter would not scorch. The reason for the long handle on the stirring paddle was to enable the person doing the stirring to stand back from the kettle far enough so that the little explosions, when bubbles of steam broke through the top of the mixture, would not throw hot bits of apple butter onto his hands and face.

The latter part of the cooking of the apple butter was the critical stage. It took considerable time, because the fire had to be kept low and the evaporation was slow. It was at this time that Elmira added the seasoning and watched carefully for the exact moment when the apple butter had been brought to perfection. Then the coals were scraped from under the big copper kettle and the apple butter was dipped into five-gallon earthen jars, sealed with paraffin, and stored. Usually at least twenty gallons were made—a year's supply. Indeed, apple butter was much prized by the members of the household.

The next special activity in the woodyard usually came in December. This was the hog butchering, which had to be done after cold weather set in. At Tarpleywick the number of hogs slaughtered depended upon the number of people regularly at the table. If there were twelve people, then twelve hogs, weighing about 220 pounds each, would be slaughtered.

First—before breakfast—two big cast iron kettles filled with water were placed on stones in the woodyard over two fires. Then the hogs were brought into the woodyard. The earlier methods of killing hogs I shall not describe, but I have a clear picture of how this was done after I was fourteen. The first act in regard to the hogs was one in which I participated with my little rifle. When the rifle cracked, the legs seemed to disappear under the hog and he dropped to the ground. Tarpley then rushed in with his butcher knife to bleed the hog by cutting the artery in its neck. As soon as the bleeding was over, the hog was placed on a platform, probably two and one-half feet high. On the ground at one end of the platform stood a large barrel sloping toward the platform. This barrel was filled with the scalding water. Two men would take hold of the hog, each one grasping a hind leg, and slide him down into the barrel, moving him up and down a little in the hot water until the hair began to slip from the skin. The hog was then brought out on the platform and the scrapers got busy taking off all of the hair and leaving the skin white and smooth. This done, a hickory stick sharpened at both ends was placed just above the hocks between the tendon and the bone. This made it possible to hang the hog, head down, on a pole supported by two forked posts. With the hog in this position it was a simple matter for Tarpley to cut straight down the belly and take out the entrails, the heart, the liver, and the lungs. At this stage the head was usually left on. The carcass was left hanging until it was well cooled. This procedure was carried on, one hog at a time. Before noon all the carcasses would be hanging from the pole.

It was quiet in the woodyard during the dinner hour, but in the afternoon there was plenty to do. The carcasses were taken down one by one and laid on a clean table where they were cut up into hams, shoulders, side meat, and fat to be rendered into lard. The fat was heated gently in the iron kettles used earlier for water. The lard extracted was dipped into large earthen jars and stored in the cool cellar. The brain and other parts of the head were made into headcheese which was put in gallon crocks and covered with hot lard.

Then there was the sausage making. After the hams, shoulders, and sides had been cut, the remaining lean meat was put through the sausage mill. It was seasoned with salt and herbs that Elmira had saved from her garden and dried for this purpose. A considerable part of this sausage was "fried down," that is, fried and put in earthen jars. This was covered with hot lard and stored away for spring and summer use. The hearts, the livers, some of the loin, the back bones, and the ribs were used as fresh meat.

The time then came for salting the hams, shoulders, and sides. This was done by putting them in barrels of brine in the cellar where they would be carefully watched until Tarpley thought they had been adequately salted. This was followed later by a turn in the smokehouse. Father put cords on each piece and hung it near the roof of the smokehouse. Then one of the big iron kettles was placed on the floor about the middle of the room. It was filled one-third full of ashes and a fire started on top of the ashes. The ashes were to keep the kettle from getting too hot on the bottom. When the fire was burning nicely, green hickory sticks were placed on top. This wood burned slowly and soon filled the room with smoke. This condition was maintained continuously until the meat had taken on a hickory flavor and the desired color. Then the hams, shoulders, and sides were taken to the outer room of the cellar and their cords were hooked over the nails on the joists.

Hog killing day was a big day. After my brother and oldest sister were married, they always came to Tarpleywick for "slaughtering" day and helped with the work. There was also a beef "slaughter" each winter, but this did not take place in the woodyard.

Once the hog killing was over, the woodyard was available for the next big event which was the accumulation of a supply of wood to last for at least a full year. Before the end of January there would be a very large pile of poles, ranging all the way from one or two inches to eight inches in diameter, on one side of the woodyard. In the days of my boyhood these poles were attacked with an axe. If the pole was of any size, a notch was chopped on one side, perhaps a little more than halfway through; then the pole was turned over and chopped in from the other side until a stick of stove length dropped loose. This was continued until the pole was cut up.

Then commenced the splitting of the wood into the size desired for the stove in which it was to be used. For the cookstove, the sticks were made rather small; two to two and one-half inches in diameter would be the largest and many of them were smaller. The bucksaw may have been used on some of the poles, but I do not recall using it. In addition, a considerable amount of wood was cut for the heating stoves. But the main thing was to have a great supply of wood for the kitchen stove which did service the year around.

February was the great month for cutting and splitting wood—before the month was over the pile of split wood for the cookstove would stand at least twenty feet high. Soon after this pile was started, an outer boundary was made by building a horseshoe-shaped "rick" about five feet high. The open end of the horseshoe was used for throwing in split wood and for taking out wood for use.

Besides the woodyard proper, there was a woodshed, a lean-to on the east side of the smokehouse. This made a woodshed sixteen feet long and eight feet wide which was filled each fall, mostly with old fence rails sawed into kitchen-stove length. I sawed most of these rails myself with a small red bucksaw—an interesting task. I would saw for a while on fence rails, and if any of them were too large for the kitchen stove, I split them. Then I would carry them in and rick them in the woodshed. I would keep at this job day after day until the woodshed was filled from one end to the other. There was a door at each end, so the shed was filled from the north end and the supply for use in the kitchen taken out at the south end.

Had I been inclined to forget this period, I would not have been allowed to because of my sister, eight years younger than I, who watched as I sawed wood. She would come out of the house with a slice of bread spread with jam, and I would say, "Carrie, this saw would go a lot faster if I had a little of your piece." Then she would take off some bread and give it to me. Then the saw would run very fast for a little while and she would laugh. As I was finishing sawing one day, she was with me in the yard, and I said, "Let's clean up all of this area so it will look nice and neat. Then, when we get it all cleaned up we'll paint it—what color?" We decided upon white. The next morning the ground was white with snow. When Carrie grew to woman-hood and had children and grandchildren, she continued to tell the story of how fast the saw would run after she gave me part of her bread and jam.

As time went on, activities at wood-sawing time changed greatly. My brother Sylvanus and John Ruby got a big steam-driven threshing outfit and used the engine in the

Steam-powered wood saw operating at home of John W. Ruby in January, 1895. Sylvanus Taylor at the rear of steam engine, John W. Ruby operating saw, H. C. Taylor throwing away the wood after it has been sawed, and others bringing logs to the saw.

wintertime for sawing wood. They bolted a circular wood saw to the front end of the engine, which made a very powerful saw—in one afternoon they would clean up a woodpile that would have taken us weeks to cut by hand.

Sawing did not finish the job on the woodpile. Many of these sawed blocks had to be split before they could be used in the heating stoves and most of them had to be split before they could be used in the cookstove. This left enough activity on the woodpile to satisfy most boys.

Two other kinds of productive activities were associated with the woodyard: the production of laundry soap and honey. The starting point for soapmaking was the ash hopper located very close to the north end of the smokehouse, between the smokehouse and the woodshed. The hopper was constructed in this way: a piece of a log about six feet long and about eight inches in diameter was hollowed out on one side to make a V-shaped trough open at one end. This was put on a solid foundation about sixteen inches from the surface of the ground at the open end and a couple of inches higher at the closed end. Then a framework about five feet long and about four feet wide was set up to hold in place the boards that were to make the hopper. One end of each board was placed in the V-shaped trough and leaned against the frame. When put into place, these boards constituted the west side and the east side of the ash hopper. Then the ends of the hopper were enclosed with boards.

During the winter, all the wood ashes from the cookstove and heating stove were put into the hopper and kept dry by a cover. When spring came, and probably before the work on the woodpile had been completed, water was poured over the top of the ashes in the hopper, and a bucket was placed under the low end of the V-shaped trough. The water went down through the ashes, leeching out the potash. This was called lye. This process of pouring water on the top and accumulating lye was continued until a large quantity of lye was in store. Then the time had come for making the soap. The big cast iron kettles were again placed in the woodyard and the lye put into the kettles. A fire was built under the kettles and the lye brought to a boil. When Elmira had tested the strength of the boiled-down lye and found it ready for dissolving the fats which she had been accumulating since hog killing time, the fats were put into the kettles with the lye. The heating continued to keep the contents of the kettles close to the boiling point until an adequate amount of fat had been dissolved for making what we called "soft soap," which was used for laundry purposes primarily but also for greasy hands. The soap—usually a year's supply— was put away in earthen jars.

The northwest corner of the woodyard, along the Osage orange hedge, was a nice place for a row of beehives. Fifteen or twenty stands of bees were kept. The whole family was interested in the bees, and although once in a while someone would get stung, it did not discourage the beekeeping. The most exciting time in connection with the bees was when a new colony in one of the hives decided to swarm. At that time of the year the menfolk would usually be in the fields, and Tarpley would be called by a wild ringing of the dinner bell which was definite notice that the bees had swarmed. He would hurry to the house and hive the bees, which by that time had come together in a very large lump of life on a limb of one of the apple trees. Tarpley was expert in getting the bees to enter an empty hive, and after a few days the hive would be added to the row of hives in the corner of the woodyard. The most important stage in the bee business was taking off the well-filled units of comb honey from the top of the hive and storing them for future use.

All the activities related to the woodyard had to do with the self-sufficient character of the farm economy. The chickens, which have been mentioned as using one corner of the woodlot, were not only a part of the farm economy but of considerable importance in the commercial economy.

Chapter Six

ORCHARDS AND GARDENS

As soon as Tarpley and Elmira commenced housekeeping at Tarpleywick they gave much attention
to producing food for the household. At first a
relatively small garden had been fenced off with spit palings;
it was southeast of the house, but as the family grew this gave
way to a half-acre garden across the road to the west. Here
raspberry, blackberry, currant, and gooseberry bushes were
planted. The rows were far enough apart so that a one-horse
double-shovel cultivator could keep the ground in good tilth
and clear of foul growth. There was also a strawberry patch
the full length of this garden. And of course there was a
great variety of vegetables. The garden was arranged so that
the ground where the annual vegetables were to be grown
could be plowed and harrowed using a team of horses, and
later the potatoes and sweet corn could be cultivated with a
one-horse double-shovel cultivator.

Some of the garden near the entrance gate was used
for special beds of lettuce, onions, various kinds of greens,
some annual flowers, and the herbs my mother used for
seasoning or for medicine. This part of the garden was cared
for with hand tools. Tarpley gave a great deal of attention
to the whole garden. I cannot enumerate all the things produced, but the fact that he grew a crop of celery impresses me
as significant. Certainly nothing was left out in the way of
small fruit and vegetables that could be produced in that
climate. Sweet potatoes, Irish potatoes, Hubbard squash,
and pumpkins were grown in large quantities outside the

garden, because there was not enough room in the garden to produce a year's supply for the house.

Tarpley planted an orchard north of the house about an acre in size. The varieties of apples were common to the 1860s; I recall especially the Red June, Maiden Blush, Snow Apple, Rambo, Russet, Genatin, Winesap, and Ben Davis. The first apples on this list were for summer and fall use and the later ones were for winter storage. Of those stored for winter the Winesap, now called "The Old-fashioned Winesap" and the Ben Davis were the most durable. The Winesap was truly a good apple. The Ben Davis was a large red apple, very coarse grained, and did not become truly edible out of hand until about May, when it was relished because no other apples were available.

Sometime in the seventies Tarpley planted an orchard to the west of the big garden. Even larger than the first one, this orchard had some new varieties of apples of which the Duchess, Jonathan, and Grimes Golden were outstanding. The Winesap had an important place in the new orchard, but no Ben Davis trees were planted. After the garden was moved across the road west of the house, the old garden east of the house was planted to peach, plum, and cherry trees—all of which added greatly to the satisfaction of the family during the summer and fall and provided the raw materials for the family canning industry.

From the beginning, the organization of the field and livestock enterprizes at Tarpleywick included something to sell, but even more attention was given to producing the food supply for the household. As time went on and the area of the farm expanded, the economy became more and more commercial. However, producing for home consumption was never lost sight of in Tarpley's day. This was the special function of the orchard and garden.

The house had a large cellar divided into two rooms. This cellar could be entered from the outside by lifting two sloping doors, going down a five-foot-wide staircase, and opening a broad door. Since the staircase and door were wide, all kinds of produce could be carried into the cellar in barrels or baskets.

A glimpse of it in early winter will attest to the great productivity of the garden and orchard. In the first room were many barrels of apples, and enough pumpkins, squash, and cabbage to last all winter and well into the spring. After the hogs had been butchered, and the hams, shoulders, and sides of bacon had been cured, the pork supply for the whole spring and summer hung from the oak joists of the ceiling.

The second room, having no outside door, was warmer. In it were large bins of Irish potatoes. (The sweet potatoes were in a box in the corner of the kitchen.) Even though they had been dried to keep all winter, they required a warmer temperature than in the cellar. Therefore in extremely cold weather, even with a fire all day in the space heater in the room above, Tarpley would sometimes take a large kettle of coals from the woodburning stove and place it in the inner room in the cellar to make sure that the potatoes would not get too cold.

This inner cellar kept much other produce, but one thing that always impressed me especially was the way Tarpley provided celery for winter use. He put a board, at least twelve inches wide, on edge on the floor about fourteen inches from the limestone wall and parallel to it. When the board was braced and fastened it formed a trench. The celery was then harvested and packed into the trench, standing as it had in the garden. Then all the interstices were filled with moist sand. As I recall, the celery was taken out a bunch at a time from one end of the trench, so that celery was on the table for several months in the winter. The parsnips were left in the ground until it thawed in the spring, and were dug for use as needed.

I cannot remember everything that was in this inner room, but onions and carrots should be mentioned. I recall also that there were shelves loaded with glass jars containing fruits, jellies, and jams. The aim was to have as many jars of preserved fruit as there were days in the year. There were also many jars of peas, string beans, and especially tomatoes and tomato juice. Standing on the floor on the south side of the inner room were several five-gallon earthen jars of cucumber pickles and some even larger earthen jars of sauerkraut.

Drying of fruits and vegetables was very important. This was done in the sunshine by placing the items to be dried on the tin roof of the porch on the south side of the house. Here sweet corn was dried in large quantities. In preparation for drying, the roasting ears were scalded and grain was sliced from the cobs. Many apples were dried on this same roof. They were peeled, cored, and sliced in preparation for drying. Navy beans and lima beans, not used when green, were permitted to dry in the pods on the vines.

The food in the cellar added to the food that came directly to the table and enabled Tarpleywick to be largely self-sufficient. Therefore, as the commercial economy of the farm continued to expand, the cash income, which in the early years had been used for buying land and farm equipment, was later available for setting up new households for the children who married, or for educating the children who chose careers other than farming. This self-sufficing economy had relaxed only slightly by 1900.

Chapter Seven

LAND USE AND CROP ROTATION

I N WRITING the history of Tarpleywick for the period from 1880 to 1900, I am dependent largely upon my own memory. Although the United States Census Schedules covering these years have been destroyed, some data for Van Buren County are available; however, I have chosen not to present this material. Instead, since I was intimately associated with Tarpleywick during all this time, I have turned to the actual Tarpleywick as my source.

Many clear pictures of those years at Tarpleywick remain in my mind. One is dated 1879, when I was six years of age. My Grandfather Martin was staying with us at that time, and I told him I wanted a straw hat. "Well," said Grandfather, "if I had some wheat straw I could make you one." So we set out to get some wheat straw. We walked up the road that runs north between sections 16 and 15 to the forty acres that Tarpley had inherited from his father. When we got there I saw a beautiful stand of wheat that had headed out, and Grandfather Martin cut the amount of wheat needed to provide straw for my hat. Thus I know that Father was farming that forty in 1879. However, before the end of the year it had been traded for the Ruby forty in section 15.

Another clear picture is my riding Old Doll hitched with another horse to a harrow. We were putting in a crop on what had been the Ruby forty the previous year.

That same year, 1880, my father purchased a hay loader. I can see myself driving the team while someone was loading the hay as it was elevated onto the wagon by the new machine. From that time on I was always associated with what-

Hayloader, similar to one purchased by Tarpley, 1880

ever was going on at Tarpleywick. By 1884 I was cultivating corn with a team and a tongueless cultivator, and in 1896 I grew my last crop at Tarpleywick, when I put in 100 acres of corn and 65 acres of oats. Even though I was away at college part of the time, I continued to be closely involved with the farm until the end of the century.

The acquisition of the land that comprised Tarpleywick from 1880 to 1900 has already been traced. Now we shall consider the use of this land. About 10 acres was devoted to lawns, gardens, orchards, and barnyards; this left about 500 acres for field crops and permanent pasture. Nearly half the 500 acres was in permanent pasture and the remainder in field crops—corn, oats, and meadows. The most valuable crop was corn, but oats, which did not pay so well, served as a nurse crop for establishing the meadows.

The ideal system of rotation was as follows: Each year about 100 acres would be in corn, 75 acres in oats, 25 acres in red clover, 25 acres in timothy and clover mixed, and 25 acres in timothy. The 25 acres of clover and timothy mixed would be left for the next year, but since the clover largely died out after the first year, it would be almost straight timothy meadow the second year.

This system was contingent upon the success of the new seeding of clover or clover and timothy mixed. When the seeding had made a stand good enough to leave, the 100

acres of corn would be planted on land which the previous
year had been used as follows: 25 acres in clover, 25 acres in
timothy, 25 acres in oats, and 25 acres in corn.

The 75 acres of oats were always planted on corn stubble. Fifty acres of this would be used as a nurse crop. Clover
was seeded with the oats on half the area and on the other
half clover and timothy mixed. This of course left 25 acres
of oats unseeded to meadow grasses.

The ideal rotation had to be readjusted when any of
the seeding for meadows failed. However, the readjustment
was always aimed at getting back to the standard rotation as
soon as possible.

Variations in the seasons resulted in fluctuations in the
quantity of corn and hay produced in any given year. The
amount of corn and hay required for the livestock each
winter was nearly constant. When, however, the pastures
were short in the autumn, the cattle had to be fed hay or
green corn fodder to supplement the pasture. Tarpley kept
this in mind and held corn and hay over from the good years
to take care of the deficits of the poor years. When the supply
of hay was inadequate some corn fodder would be cut and
shocked to supplement the hay for winter feeding. He always
had enough corn to carry his spring pigs until the new corn
crop was available. I recall one year when neighbors came
and begged Tarpley to sell them some corn out of his "ever-
normal" granary. They offered him a dollar a bushel, which
would be the equivalent of five dollars a bushel today. At
that price he sold what he could spare, but he did not make
a practice of selling corn. He did sell oats that remained
in the bins after the horses and the sheep had had their
annual quota, so that the oat bins would be empty and swept
clean before threshing time.

In planning his rotation of crops, Tarpley kept in mind
not only the efficient use of the soil to provide feed for his
livestock but also the demand made for man and horse labor.
It was important that there not be high peaks of demand for
labor at certain times during the growing season and low demand at other times. The use of labor was carefully sched-
uled in the plan adopted at Tarpleywick. The oats and
accompanying grass seeds were planted in April, before the
land was warm enough for planting corn. The tenth of April
was looked upon as the time to sow oats. The plowing and

"fitting" of the land for corn needed to be finished by the tenth of May, which was considered the best time to plant corn. More important than this date was the condition of the weather and the soil. Generally, the oat seeding and the corn planting supplemented each other perfectly in the use of man and horse labor.

When all the crops had been planted, the oats and hay required no further attention until harvesttime, but the cornfields had to be kept clean of weeds and grasses if there was to be a good crop. They needed cultivating at least three times and were sometimes cultivated five times. There was some conflict between corn cultivation and harvesting clover hay. Because these two activities overlapped, it was very important to be able to reduce the corn cultivation to a minimum by keeping the soil as free as possible of weed seeds.

The corn was cultivated for the last time, or "laid-by," when it was from knee-high to hip-high. After it was laid-by some weeds and grasses would grow, so Tarpley turned his spring lambs into the cornfields about the time the corn was in tassel and too large to be tempting to the lambs. These lambs ranged all over the cornfields and ate the ragweeds, foxtails, and other weeds and grasses that had sprung up. The weeds and grasses were thus kept from going to seed and the fields were kept relatively clean. This was especially important if the spring had been wet and it had been difficult to keep the cornfields clean because the ground had been too wet to be cultivated. It also meant that fewer cultivations would be required the following year, which was important, as we have seen, because clover hay harvest was competitive with corn cultivation.

The mixed clover and timothy hay was usually harvested after the corn had been laid-by and before harvesting oats. If some of the timothy meadow was to be cut for seed, it followed the oat harvest. The oats and timothy seed were threshed by an itinerant threshing machine which usually spent three days at Tarpleywick. As soon as the oat shocks were dry enough, threshing started. The crew was made up of neighbors who exchanged labor at threshing time. This meant that after the threshing was done at Tarpleywick, many days were spent helping the neighbors.

Following the "round robin" of helping the neighbors with threshing came a period for making vacation trips and catching up on all kinds of work that needed to be done—especially repairing buildings and fences and hauling manure. Manure hauling was especially important because during the busy season it accumulated near the horse barn, and the cattle barns and sheep sheds had to be cleaned in preparation for the coming winter. Many days of work were required to clean out all of this manure and to spread it on the land which was to be in corn the following year. Tarpley never owned a mechanical manure spreader. In those days the spreading of manure was done with a skillful flick of the long-handled four-pronged pitchfork that would scatter a forkful over about a yard of area—a time-consuming procedure. There were three reasons for spreading manure in the fall: It used the farm labor effectively, it got the barns and sheds ready to house the cattle and sheep for the winter, and it insured having the manure on the ground that was to be plowed for corn the following spring. This would seem to be the time to point out that in the forty years he farmed, Tarpley used no commercial fertilizers.

As soon as the corn was mature enough to be cribbed, cornhusking was the order of the day. This often ran from mid-October to well into November. With the husking of the corn, the crop year ended and no more field work would be done until the following spring.

A great variety of work was carried out during the winter months, some of which is described in the chapter on "Woodyard Activities." Tarpley did not keep a notebook, as I have known other farmers to do, listing odd jobs to be done in winter or when the land was too wet to be worked in the summertime. He apparently had the whole picture of the farm and labor requirements so clearly in mind that he did not need a notebook. He never was without something for the workers to do, regardless of the weather or the condition of the land.

Chapter Eight

SEEDING AND CULTIVATION

I n 1861, when Tarpley Early Taylor started farming for himself, the mouldboard plow was in common use. The one he bought had a twelve-inch plowshare which could be taken off for sharpening at a blacksmith shop. It was drawn by two horses, the beam and handles were wooden, and the depth of plowing could be regulated by adjusting the clevices. This particular plow turned the soil to the left and was called a left-handed plow. Tarpley used this plow for plowing the land, whether it was meadow, wheat stubble, or corn stubble, although plows with different shaped mouldboards were available for plowing sod.

Once the ground had been plowed, the surface had to be smoothed and pulverized by means of a harrow. The common harrow of that time was a homemade affair shaped like an **A** with steel teeth about ten inches long which any blacksmith could make. These teeth were usually square but sometimes round. They extended about six inches below the wooden frame and were drawn to a sharp point at the lower end. This type of harrow would smooth a strip about seven feet wide and was used at Tarpleywick for many years.

When Tarpley started farming, he may have used a

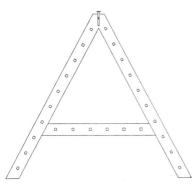

"A" harrow made by Tarpley with the help of a blacksmith who made the teeth. It was used by Tarpley for at least twenty years.

53

brush harrow made by taking two medium-sized thorn bushes, trimming them so they were somewhat flat on one side, then fastening their butts together with a chain to which a team of horses could be hitched. This type of brush harrow did a very good job of smoothing and pulverizing the land and was occasionally used in the late seventies at Tarpleywick when an extra harrow was needed.

Planting corn in 1861 has already been described. Not many years later a method was introduced that enabled the farmer to cultivate the corn lengthwise and crosswise of the field. The land to be planted was marked off in squares about forty-two inches on each side, with a homemade marker which would make three parallel marks. It had a tongue and a neck yoke so arranged that the horses, hitched one on each side of the tongue, would keep the marker from wobbling as it moved across the field. The farmer marked off the field by driving first over the whole field in one direction and then going over the whole field crosswise.

Two methods were used for planting corn in this carefully marked field. It could be done by taking a hoe, digging a small hole at the cross made by the marker, dropping in three or four seeds of corn, and covering them with the hoe, or by using a hand planter which had been developed prior to 1860. This planter enabled the farmer to plant a row of corn as fast as he could walk. The planter consisted of two four-inch boards about three and one-half feet long with metal points about three inches long below the wood. The two boards were placed facing each other with the metal points on the inside. The boards were hinged together above the points. To enclose the space between the two boards, just above the hinge, canvas or some other flexible material had been fastened to the edges of the boards while they were pulled apart at the top. A handle had been placed on each of these boards near the top. The farmer took hold of these two handles, with which the tops of the boards could be pulled apart or pushed together. When the tops were pushed together, the metal points were open, but when the tops were

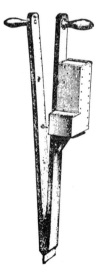

Hand corn planter used in the early days for planting corn and in later days for replanting missing hills.

Brown's corn planter

apart the two metal points were brought together so that the planter could be set in the ground. A box, a foot or more long, was attached to one of the boards and held the seed corn. Fastened to the opposite board was a device that slipped into the bottom of the corn box when the boards were pushed together at the top. When the handles were pulled apart this brought out three or four seeds of corn and dropped them down between the metal points, ready to go into the ground. When the handles at the top were pushed together, the points separated and the seeds dropped into the ground. The farmer would then withdraw the points of the planter as he moved forward and close the hole made by the planter with a stroke of his right foot. At the same time he would draw the handles apart and set the point of the planter in the next cross. A skillful operator could plant one hill after another without hesitation. This method was much more rapid than the hoe, but a skillful farmer could plant a lot of corn in a day using either the hoe or the hand planter. Both methods were used at Tarpleywick.

Sometime in the seventies a two-row corn planter was purchased. This planter was painted blue, but it was called "The Brown Corn Planter" since it was named for the maker. With this machine the field had to be marked off beforehand only crosswise to the direction of planting. The planter had two wheels with iron tires about six inches wide which were concave so that they pressed the soil toward the center. In front of each wheel was a runner, about three feet long, called a shoe. It tapered to a thin blade at the front end, but at the back end it spread out about an inch and one-half at the heel so that it opened the soil for the seed.

About sixteen inches above this heel, on each side of the planter, was a seed box. A shaft running from the bottom of one seed box to the bottom of the other activated a device for dropping seeds. A board about eight inches wide ran from the top of one seed box to the top of the other. A lever

extended up from the activating shaft through this board.
On this board a small person, even a ten or twelve year old
boy or girl, would sit and operate the lever. As the heels of
the shoes crossed a marker line, the lever would be pulled
to drop the seeds. At the next marker line the lever would
be pushed in the opposite direction to drop the seeds.

My oldest sister Laura used to help my father plant
corn. A team of horses would be hitched to the "Brown"
planter, and with Tarpley in the driver's seat and Laura on
the board between the boxes, it would move at a steady pace
across the field. The click-clack, click-clack of the machine
would beat out an even rhythm from one end of the field
to the other as my sister operated the lever. She had a repu-
tation of dropping the seeds right on the marker line.

As was mentioned earlier in this chapter, the corn was
planted on evenly spaced cross marks so that it could be
cultivated in both directions. After this improvement in
the technique of planting, the practice of hoeing corn ended.
However, in the eighties I sometimes found myself going
through a cornfield and pulling weeds out of the hills in
especially weedy spots.

Sometime in the eighties a mechanical method of dropping the corn was attached to the "Brown" corn planter,
making it unnecessary to mark off the land. The attachment
was activated by a wire with little balls on it which were
spaced forty-two inches apart. This wire was first unrolled
along the edge of the field, from one end of the field to the
other, and fastened securely at each end with an iron stake.
The planter was driven into position and the wire placed
in the runnel of the device which had been attached to the
shaft going to the corn boxes. This device did the work that
had previously been done by a small person operating the
hand lever. As the planter moved across the field and the
wire ran through the slot, the balls on the wire tripped the
shaft and seeds were dropped every forty-two inches. A
sharp click would tell the farmer that a ball on the wire had
tripped the corn boxes. At the end of the row the wire was
released from the planter. The team and planter were
turned around into position for the next rows. The farmer
would then reset the stake holding the wire, place the wire in
the runnel, and start across the field again. If the right ten-
sion was maintained on the wire while each pair of rows

Double-shovel cultivator

was being planted, the rows were as straight crosswise as lengthwise of the field and could be cross-cultivated. The wire was called a "check-wire," the attachment a "check-row attachment." This old "Brown" planter, with this same check-row device was still in use in 1896 when I planted my last crop of corn. A farmer had to be skillful to do a perfect job of check-row planting.

The early method of corn cultivation has been described in Chapter 2. The single-shovel cultivator was soon replaced by the double-shovel cultivator, which had two shanks, one on each side of the beam, with a shovel on each shank. One of the shovels was six or eight inches farther back than the other. These shovels were about four inches wide, although sometimes narrower and sometimes broader. This cultivator, drawn by one horse, enabled the farmer to cultivate one row of corn each round, thus cutting down by one-third the amount of travel required when the single-shovel was used. Someone later invented the tongueless cultivator which enabled one man to handle two double-shovel cultivators.

The tongueless cultivator had an iron frame shaped like an inverted U or arch with horizontal projections on either side and was mounted on two wheels. The inverted U in the center permitted it to straddle a row of corn three feet high and to draw two double-shovel cultivators, one on each side attached to the horizontal projection between each leg of the arch and the wheel. Each wheel was mounted on a casting fastened to the end of the frame by a vertical pin which allowed it to make approximately a quarter turn to the right or left. The front of this casting had an extension to which a singletree was attached. Even though each double-shovel cultivator had only one handle, it was stabilized by the front

Typical tongueless cultivator

attachment to the frame. However, a cooperative team of horses was needed for use on this implement. A horse was hitched to each singletree and the farmer was ready to start across the field straddling a row of corn, manipulating each double-shovel cultivator with one hand, and thus cultivating both sides of the row at the same time.

For moving the tongueless cultivator on the road or from field to field, a dragbar could be pulled backward to the ground from the casting on which the wheels were attached, and could be fastened in that position by tightening a wing nut. Then the two double shovels were hung on arms reaching back from the arch.

The tongueless cultivator used at Tarpleywick carried the name "The New Departure" and was sold by Lamson at Fairfield. The genius of this cultivator, as of all cultivators made for cultivating row crops since that day, was in the fact that the hitch of the front end of the beam of the double shovel to the framework had two joints, one that would allow the double shovel to be moved up and down by a single handle and another joint that would enable the operator to move the double shovel to the right or the left in order to maintain right relations with the row of corn even though the team of horses failed to straddle the row perfectly. It was very important that this double shovel should have no other directions of motion because the operator was continually watching to make sure of the right relation of the double shovels to the corn. If there were any "wobble" in the double shovel this could not be done with one handle. This principle has been carried forward as the first essential in all of the varieties of corn cultivators, whether they were one-row, two-row, or eight-row cultivators.

The two handles of this tongueless cultivator were bent to the left enough so the operator could walk on the left side of the row of corn while guiding the two double shovels. As a boy I developed the practice of using my left hip to push the handle of the left double shovel to the left as I drew the right double shovel over toward the row with my right hand. This relieved my left arm of a tiresome task of reaching straight down from the shoulder and pushing the handle to the left in adjusting the double shovels to the row of corn. This position of the operator facilitated the use of the right foot, in my case a bare foot, in uncovering any small corn

Tongued one-row corn culti-
vator which replaced the
tongueless cultivator.

plant that may have been covered up by the earth thrown by one of the shovels.

About the turn of the century a tongue was fastened to the top of the inverted arch on the tongueless cultivator, and the method of hitching the horses was changed. This cultivator is only slightly different from the tongueless cultivator described above. The importance of the development of the tongueless cultivator was that one man could do the work of two with the new implement. As to the date of the introduction of the tongueless cultivator, I know that it was in use at Tarpleywick when I became aware of what was going on in the cornfields. It is the cultivator I used from 1884, when I first cultivated corn, to 1896, when I grew my last crop.

It will be recalled that Tarpley's land area had been greatly enlarged in 1879. Because of the greater area of tillage land, he was looking for laborsaving devices, so about this time he bought a sulky turning plow with a sixteen-inch bottom drawn by three horses. This plow was called a gang plow when it had two or more bottoms. It was made entirely of iron, with the exception of the tongue and the neckyoke. This plow was used for many years at Tarpleywick, although I have no memory of ever using it myself. I preferred walking plows; in 1896, with the help of one boy, I raised 100 acres of corn—all with two three-horse mouldboard walking plows with sixteen-inch shares.

Oats were usually seeded where corn had been grown the year before and the ground was not turned with a mouldboard plow. The common practice was to loosen the soil

Tarpley's sulky plow looked
something like this. It had
one sixteen-inch bottom in-
stead of the two twelve-inch
bottoms shown and it was
drawn by three horses, not
four. Sulky plows having
more than one bottom were
called gang plows.

with a corn cultivator, sow the seed broadcast, and then harrow it into the ground. This broadcast seeding was long done
by hand, but sometime in the eighties the endgate seeder was
invented and Tarpley got one of them. This machine consisted of a hopper that would hold about a bushel of seed
grain and had a device at the bottom that would whirl at a
high speed and spread the seed over a strip twelve or fifteen
feet wide. The spreading device was put in place of the endgate at the rear of a wagon box. A sprocket wheel was attached to the right rear wheel of the wagon and it propelled
a chain that operated a small sprocket wheel on a shaft which
at the other end was geared to the whirling device that cast
the seed. No drill for seeding small grain was used at
Tarpleywick in Tarpley's day.

Oats were used as a nurse crop for timothy and clover.
After the oats had been seeded and harrowed once, clover
seed, or a mixture of timothy and clover seed, was sowed. In
the earlier years, certainly well into the eighties, this was
done by hand by a man carrying a bag of seed slung from
his shoulder. In later days, a wheelbarrow seeder with
a seed box ten or twelve feet long was filled with the desired
mixture of seed. A device set in motion by the turning of the
metal wheel activated a slide in the bottom of the seed box
so that the seeds dropped to the ground. This was an improvement, not only because the farmer could sow a wider
strip but because an evener job of seeding could be done.
The timothy seed especially was so light that if there was
much wind it took great skill to seed evenly when the seeds
were cast by hand. After the timothy and clover seeds were
on the ground, the field was harrowed crosswise to cover the
seeds. This was facilitated in the early eighties when a new
type of harrow was introduced at Tarpleywick.

The new harrow was made up of three sections, each
having three bars about five feet long. These bars were made
of wood and each carried five or six teeth. This harrow was
drawn on a slight angle so that no two teeth would be in line
with each other. This kind of harrow took various forms
and could be made by the farmer who had carpenter skills,
with the aid of a blacksmith to make the teeth. Tarpley's
first section harrow was purchased from the machinery dealer
and had a patented device for hinging the sections together
which was later discarded. The section harrow was still in
use at the end of the century.

One change in the method of seeding small grain at Tarpleywick was introduced in the late eighties or early nineties when the disc replaced the tongueless corn cultivator for loosening up the soil in the cornfields of the previous year. This made a somewhat better seedbed and cut up the stalks left from the previous year and got them out of the way so that they did not interfere with harvesting the oats or the clover and timothy crops that followed.

Another machine Tarpley had for preparing the land was especially important when corn was to be grown two years in a row on the same land. This was a cornstalk cutter. It consisted of a two-wheeled outfit with a tongue and wheels. Between the wheels was a chopping device consisting of a rotating cylinder with five chopping blades horizontal to the direction of movement. This was weighted so that as it rolled forward it would chop the stalks of the last year's corn crop into short pieces. It was of course not needed where the corn had been cut for fodder, but most of the corn at Tarpleywick was husked in the field and the stalks left standing.

Occasionally a roller was used for crushing clods on the surface of a field. It consisted of a wooden log seven feet long and about eighteen inches in diameter, carved to an even diameter and having a smooth surface from end to end. A steel pin about an inch and one-half in diameter was placed in the center of each end. To these pins a frame was attached which had a tongue so that a team could be hitched to it. There was also a seat for a driver. This roller was sometimes used after the corn had come up and before the first cultivation in case there were many clods on the surface of the field.

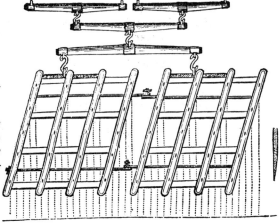

This section harrow was like the one Tarpley bought in 1880 excepting his harrow had three sections hinged together with three bars each.

HARVEST

DURING THE EARLY YEARS of Tarpley's farming at Tarpleywick, all the hay was cut with a scythe. After a given area had been cut it had to be gone over by a man with a pitchfork who tossed the heavy bunches of hay so that it would all dry evenly. When the hay was dry enough it was raked by hand with a wooden rake and put into cocks with a pitchfork so that it could finish curing. After it was well cured in the cock it was hauled to the barnyard. During the very early days at Tarpleywick it was stacked close to the horse shed, but in a few years Tarpley built a barn with adequate haymows for storing enough hay for all the livestock sheltered in the barn.

As the farm was enlarged it became the habit to stack some of the hay in the fields and to feed it to the cattle by putting enough for one day's feeding on a wagon rack and scattering it in small bunches on the ground in the general neighborhood of the stack. This method of feeding cattle

This wooden hay rake was drawn by one horse and the operator walked behind. The wooden teeth ran under the hay and when it was time to dump the rake the operator pushed up on the handles, the rake turned over leaving the windrow behind and the other set of teeth slipped under the hay in the swath to pick up hay enough for a windrow.

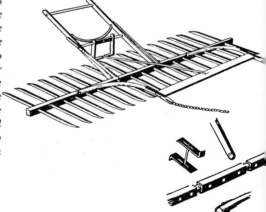

in the winter was brought from Kentucky by Tarpley's father, William Early Taylor.

Just how soon the scythe gave way to a mowing machine is not known, but sometime before 1870 a mowing machine drawn by two horses was introduced. This mower was in combination with a reaping machine for wheat and oats and will be described later. About this time a wooden hay rake was acquired. Several years later a steel-toothed hay rake mounted on wheels and drawn by one horse replaced the wooden rake.

The mowing machine and the rake changed the procedure for making hay. The mowed grass was left lying in the swath until cured; then it was raked into windrows and put onto a wagon with a three-pronged long-handled pitchfork. Usually two men pitched the hay onto the wagon and one man on the wagon carefully loaded it. For hauling hay, the wagon was equipped with a rack sixteen feet long and eight feet wide, called a hayrack, which provided a large level base for a load of hay. It required skill to build a fine big load that would not shift on the way to the barn.

The first barn built at Tarpleywick had a ramp so that a load of hay could be driven into the center bent of the mow and unloaded by hand by men using long-handled pitchforks. The hay was pitched from the wagon and then carried back into the mow a forkful at a time. However, a horse-drawn hayfork was soon installed in the barn; this hoisted the hay from the load to a carrier that ran on a track along the length of the crest of the barn. Just when this device was put in is not known, but it is certain that all during the eighties and nineties it was used in all the barns

This steel-toothed hay rake was used for many years by Tarpley before he got the hay loader (p. 49). After he got the hay loader he sometimes raked the hay into small windrows before picking it up with the hay loader.

I remember the "Old Manny" which my father disposed of about 1875 as looking just like this.

at Tarpleywick. With this fork a skillful operator could unload a large load of hay in five forkfuls. Each forkful would be hoisted to the crest of the barn, carried along the track to the mow, and dropped close to the spot where it was to be mowed away. Usually one horse provided the power for the operation of this fork. The job of riding this horse and controlling it could be done nicely by an eight- or ten-year-old child and was a treat to the child who loved horses.

The next improvement in haymaking came with the hay-loader which Tarpley acquired in 1880. This machine was attached to the back end of the wagon carrying the hay-rack. As the horses pulled the wagon forward, the hay-loader would pick up the hay from the two mower swaths, push it up a smooth sloping structure, elevating it to the height of a big load of hay, and drop it on the back end of the hayrack. In this way a fine big load of hay could be put on the wagon by one man and a small boy who drove the team. The man would build his load in an orderly manner, starting at the front of the rack while the boy guided the team over the swaths. I remember driving the team when I was seven years of age. In case the hay was thin on the ground in a dry year, it would be raked into small windrows, so that the loader could pick it up with less driving. Thus the hay-loader enabled a man and a boy to do a job which formerly had taken three men and a boy.

The mower, the hay-loader, and the horsepower hayfork in the barn, continued to be the approved equipment for making hay as long as Tarpley farmed, to the end of the nineteenth century.

Small grain was cut with a grain cradle scythe for several years at Tarpleywick. This tool was a scythe with a longer blade than was used for mowing hay. It had a set of fingers, mounted on the snath above the blade, that held the grain that was cut as the scythe was swung from right to left. At the end of the swing of the cradle the cut grain was laid in a swath to the left. This was not easy work and required a high degree of skill. The grain in the swath might be raked into bunches by means of a large wooden hand rake. Where the grain was a good stand, so that the swath provided a bundle every two or three feet, the rake was not used. Tarpley's method was to roll up enough for a sheaf by shifting his feet along under the cut grain until he had enough for a bundle. He would then reach down, pick up the sheaf, put the band around it, and fasten the ends by twisting and tucking them under the band. The bundle was then tossed aside and the next bundle was made in the same manner. A skillful man could perform this act in much briefer time than is required to tell it.

These bundles were later set up into shocks. After the grain was well cured in the shocks, it might be hauled to the barnyard or to some other point where a strawpile was wanted; there it was put into waterproof stacks or ricks to await the coming of the itinerant threshing machine. If the threshing machine could be obtained at the right time, the farmer would thresh directly from the shock. This was Tarpley's usual practice. Timothy for seed was cut, bound, shocked, and usually threshed from the shock.

Sometime in the latter part of the 1860s Tarpley acquired a reaping machine which was a combined reaper and mower. It was called "The Old Manny." When I was a very small child—in 1875 or 1876—Father took me with him to the field where "The Old Manny" was standing. He was selling this machine to two farmers who had continued to use the cradle up to that time.

"The Old Manny" had a sickle bar, probably five feet long, which had a sickle operated by gears driven by the wheels as the machine was drawn forward by two horses. When used as a mower this simple equipment sufficed, but for cutting grain a reel was put in use and a platform was attached to the rear edge of the cutter bar onto which the reel placed the grain as it was cut. It normally took two men to operate this machine, one to drive the team and

Old Reliable McCormick reaping machine which Tarpley purchased when he sold the "Old Manny."

another, sitting on a second seat, to use a long-handled pitchfork with which he raked the grain from the platform as often as enough had accumulated to make a good sized bundle. Tarpley had his horses trained well enough so that he could sit on the raker's seat and also drive the team.

It was certainly not later than 1876 that Tarpley sold "The Old Manny" and bought "The Old Reliable" McCormick self-rake mowing and reaping machine. As a mower this machine had its own cutter bar, four feet long, with a sickle that could be sharpened on a grindstone. This machine, like "The Old Manny," was drawn by two horses when used as a mower and by three horses when used as a reaper.

When used as a reaping machine a longer cutter bar with a bearded sickle was used and there was a wheel at the outer end of the cutter bar. Back of the cutter bar was a platform. There was a reel to knock the cut grain straight back on the platform. Associated with the reel was a cleverly devised rake which synchronized with the reel as it passed toward the sickle bar and then made a circular movement for a fourth of a circle with its teeth on the platform so it raked the accumulated grain from the platform and dropped it on the ground behind the driver's seat. It then changed to a vertical movement until it was past vertical when it changed its course adequately to synchronize with the reel. This was an excellent machine and served well for many years.

In 1882 Tarpley bought a self-binding reaping machine. This was a twine binder with the Appleby knotter. This new machine largely replaced the McCormick self-rake machine as a reaper, but the McCormick mower held its position on the farm for several years. I recall that as late as two years after the self-binder had come into use at Tarpleywick, the "Old Reliable" McCormick reaper was requisitioned to supplement the binder in harvesting the timothy cut for seed. I remember this well for I suggested that this be done. Tarpley operated the reaper, and a hired man and I did the binding and at the same time the shocking of the timothy bundles. After several years the McCormick mower became badly worn and Tarpley purchased a new mower. No addi-

The self-binding reaping machine which Tarpley bought in 1882.

Tarpley's new mower purchased in the late 1880s.

Horsepower threshing outfit. Note tumbling rod as it approaches separator.

tional equipment for harvesting was procured before the end of the century.

From the beginning of his farming career to the end of the century Tarpley had his threshing done by an itinerant threshing machine. For the greater part of the thirty years from 1861 to 1891, the threshing was done by a horsepower machine. The horsepower consisted of a four-wheeled framework carrying a large set of heavy gears under a platform on which the operator stood. Five heavy beams, equally distant apart, extended from the edges of this platform. A team was hitched to the outer end of each of these beams and the hitch strap of each horse was fastened to the beam in front. These five teams were kept moving steadily in a circle by the man with a whip in his hand standing on the platform of this horsepower. From the lower part of the horsepower a rod about an inch and one-half in diameter was attached to the gears. It angled down almost to the ground before reaching to the path of the horses where there was a universal joint which we then called a "knuckle" and a bearing block staked to the ground. From there the rod ran parallel and close to the ground so the horses could easily step over it. After clearing the path of the horses there was another bearing and a universal joint. From that point the rod, with proper supports, angled upward to the front part of the outfit called the separator, which consisted of the cylinder which whipped the seed from the straw and the shakers and riddles which separated the straw and the chaff from the seeds. At the upper end of this rod, which was commonly called the "tumbling rod," was a large cog wheel, which I remember as being fifteen or sixteen inches in diameter, and to which the tumbling rod was attached. This, as I recall, was at the right side of the front end of the separator as one stood at the horsepower and looked at the machine. This gear, which was opposite the cylinder which whipped out the grain, activated a small pinion on the right end of the shaft of the cylinder. While the horses moved slowly, the gears speeded up the tumbling rod and the large gear on the end of the tumbling rod multiplied the speed manyfold so that the cylinder ran at a very high speed. Since this heavy cylinder could not be stopped suddenly when the power ceased to be applied, there was a ratchet between the small pinion and the cylinder. In later automobile days it was called a "freewheeling" device. The ratchet made a loud click when the cylinder was running free and I recall that that clicking sound could yet be heard when the threshing was stopped at dinnertime in the middle of the day and we had gone twenty rods or more from the machine toward the house.

It took a good-sized crew to do the threshing; four or five men with their bundle wagons to bring the grain from the shocks to the separator, two men in the field to pitch the bundles onto the wagons, one man to cut the bands as the bundles were placed on the feeding table by the man on a bundle wagon, a man to measure the grain or seed and place it in the wagon box if it was oats and in sacks if it was timothy seed, two or three men on the straw pile, and at least one man to haul the grain from the machine to the bin in the barn. All the men operating the machinery were provided by the owner of the machine. This included, besides the man on the horsepower, two men who took turns feeding the loose bundles into the cylinder. This required skill. The crew provided by the farmer was made up of men and boys from the neighbors who exchanged labor at threshing time. If all the conditions were favorable, Tarpley's threshing could be done in three days in the 1880s.

At dinnertime the house was a busy place. Neighbor

Steam-power threshing outfit between jobs

women came in to help Elmira and her daughters with the work of preparing and serving the meal. The table usually had to be set a second time in order that everybody could be seated. Tarpley provided fresh meat for these occasions by butchering an animal: usually a sheep, but sometimes a calf or a pig. When the crew arrived for dinner they found pails of water along with several wash pans on a long bench in the yard for the men to clean up for dinner. The cooks had no occasion to complain that the men lacked' good appetites!

Sometime in the 1890s horsepower was replaced by a steam engine. The power was transmitted from the engine to the separator by means of a belt six inches wide running over a pulley attached to the cylinder shaft of the separator. This pulley was much smaller than the belt wheel on the engine in order that the speed of the cylinder would be much faster than the belt wheel on the engine. Coal or wood was used as fuel for the engine and the farmer was expected to provide the fuel.

The general practice at Tarpleywick was to husk the corn from the standing stalks in the field. The only equipment was a team and wagon with the sideboards on the wagon box. If one person was husking alone he would have a two- or three-foot bangboard on the right side of the wagon. He would then husk two rows at a time with the wagon and team straddling the last row which had been previously husked. On his right hand he would have a husking peg, or he might have husking gloves with a husking peg attached to the right glove. The team was controlled by voice and the husker kept his eye on the rows of corn, taking an ear of corn out of the husk and loosening it from the stem in about three quick motions and tossing it into the wagon box without looking. Hence the importance of the bangboard. When three persons were following one wagon, five rows were taken with the team straddling the center row, one person husking two rows on one side, another the two rows on the other side, and the third person following and husking out the row that had been straddled. In this case the bangboard had to be removed. I did most of my cornhusking alone. With a good crop I would fill the wagon box, with the corn heaped up against the bangboard, twice a day. This meant at least fifty-five bushels per day. I once tried husking three loads a day but that proved too strenuous. Each load was taken from the field and shovelled into the corncrib. In trying to get three loads a day the unloading time did not fit with mealtimes.

Tarpley made a practice of "hogging down" one field, usually not more than ten acres, as soon as the corn was in the dent. If most of the hogs were only half grown and found it difficult to break down the stalks to get access to the ears, some old sows were put in with them for riding down the stalks. This method of harvesting the corn enabled the farmer to start in on the new crop without the labor of snapping off the ears and hauling them to the feedlot. It also left the hog manure on the field. It gave the hogs more exercise than was consistent with economical feeding in the latter part of the preparation of the hogs for market. However, it fitted in well with Tarpley's extensive type of farming.

When corn was cut for fodder, a corn knife with a blade about eighteen inches long and a handle about six inches long was used. No corn binder was used at Tarpleywick in Tarpley's day, and the day of the cornhusking machine of the modern type, either one or two row, had not come.

Chapter Ten

LIVESTOCK

HORSES, CATTLE, HOGS, AND SHEEP were all important in the livestock economy at Tarpleywick in the period from 1880 to 1900.

The number of horses expanded to more than twenty and reached a maximum of twenty-six at one time. This included one team of mules for most of the period and there was always one driving team of light weight (about 1,100 pounds) that was used on the road hitched to the spring wagon or in the fields for lighter work. In those days the power used on the farm was provided entirely by horses and was thus a part of the self-sufficing economy. The horses not only furnished the farm power and drew the vehicles on the road but they also provided a continuous supply of draft animals for the market, thus adding very materially to the cash income. This is one of the striking differences between the farm economy of the eighties and nineties of the nineteenth century, and that of the nineteen fifties.

Beef cattle of the English shorthorn type were bred and reared on Tarpleywick farm. From thirty to forty brood cows were maintained as the breeding herd, and the offspring were usually put in the market at about two and one-half years of age, although of course some of the heifers were turned into the breeding herd and some of the older members of the breeding herd were fattened and sold each year. While a high percentage of the food for the cattle came from the pastures and the hay consumed in the winter months, they were corn fed during the latter months of their stay on the farm so as to be sold as fat corn-fed cattle. The aim was to have two carloads of beef cattle for the market each year.

In the late 1870s a market for cream developed in the Tarpleywick area, so Tarpley decided to give more emphasis to milk production by topcrossing his English shorthorn cows with a Holstein bull. He had been led to believe that this would not only greatly increase the milk yield but that the male calves would make good beef steers. This was tried out for only a few years. While it increased the income from butterfat, the half-bred Holstein steers proved too leggy and rough in appearance at two and one-half years of age and did not sell well in the beef market so he returned to the use of a shorthorn sire.

One amusing incident in connection with this Holstein episode was the comment of Jake Rocky. He and his wife and two boys lived on a forty-acre farm on the righthand side of the road three-quarters of a mile east of the Tarpleywick residence. The father and the boys exhibited a great interest in what they considered the right use of words. For instance, if you pointed out a fine mare and said, "We think that a very fine horse," they would respond, "That is not a horse, it is a mare." They thought the term *horse* applied only to the males of that species and would say, "A hoss is a hoss but a mare isn't a hoss," and there was no use arguing with them. When my father introduced the Holstein sire and the black and white calves began to appear in large numbers on Tarpleywick farm, we called them Holsteins, but the Rockys, father and sons, objected and said, "Those aren't Holsteins, they're only Halfsteins."

Hogs were a very important source of income. From twelve to fourteen brood sows were kept, half of which were old sows and about half gilts. The old sows, after producing a litter of spring pigs and nursing them to weening time, were fattened and sold. The young sows were usually bred for fall litters and kept over to the next spring for a third crop of pigs. This means more than a hundred hogs could be sent to the market each year, in addition to those that were slaughtered for home use.

Ear corn was usually fed to the hogs in Tarpley's day. They made good use of it. But the corn, even of that day, with a protein content of about 9 percent, provided too much starch and not enough protein to make the best type of hog for cured meat production. They were too fat and did not carry an adequate proportion of lean meat. Tarpley remedied this in some measure by feeding his growing hogs a considerable amount of slop made of ground rye or other small grains. At that time the hogs were being bred so that they were losing their bacon-hog conformation characteristic of the breed that had been introduced from the Canton, China, area and known in Iowa as the Poland-China breed. As a small boy I was acquainted with the spotted Poland-China, but in the nineties they were not seen on Iowa farms. Since the buyers representing the slaughterhouses were paying no more for bacon type hogs than for the lard type hog, they were quite generally fed on corn alone.

Since the hog farmer was usually a beef cattle farmer, it was a common practice to always have a goodly number of growing hogs following the cattle in the feed lot. There are at least two good reasons why hog feeding in Iowa has changed in recent years. The buyers for the slaughterhouses are preferring the bacon type hogs to the lard type hog and paying a better price for the bacon type than for the lard type. Another reason is that the large yields of hybrid corn carry about 7 percent protein instead of 9 percent protein and hence require a greater supplement in order to produce a bacon type hog.

Sheep continued to be very important at Tarpleywick. About three hundred ewes was the maximum number kept through each winter in the later years of this period. They were not purebreds but French Merino grades. The flock was always maintained by associating the ewes with purebred rams of the French Merino type. Sheep shearing was always an important event immediately after corn planting or even on wet-weather days during corn planting time. This job could fit in with the work in the cornfields in large measure between corn planting and the first cultivation of the corn. The ewes did not shear very heavy fleeces (from six to nine pounds) but the Merino rams sheared as high as twenty-five pounds.

Each year the older ewes, those that had failed to lamb the previous spring, the male lambs, and the ewe lambs that were not held to replenish the breeding flock, were fattened and sold in the autumn. Lamb and mutton were available for the dining table at Tarpleywick. The self-sufficing economy was practiced for most of the meat supply up to 1900.

Poultry was important at Tarpleywick in that it provided eggs for the market, fryers for the dining table, and eggs to supplement the bacon or ham on the breakfast table. There were usually some turkeys and some geese. Thanksgiving was celebrated with a turkey, and New Years with a goose. The geese, furthermore, gave up their breast feathers each spring to supply materials for featherbeds.

With all this livestock supplying food for the family and for the market, it might be thought that the cash income of Tarpleywick would be rather large, but in dollars it was not imposing. My father did not keep detailed accounts, but I recall that in the nineties he told me one year that he sold about $2,000 worth of products. That figure looks very small when compared with C. A. Warner's $21,000 in 1965.

To evaluate this figure one needs to keep in mind that hogs and beef cattle were selling for about two and one-half cents a pound, sheep for a little less, the price of wool was nine cents a pound, and it took an extra good horse to bring $100. But along with those low prices it is important to remember that a young man or a young woman could attend Drake University in Des Moines or the Iowa State College at Ames and his total expenses, including his traveling expenses between his home and the college, were easily met by $200, and that a schoolteacher in the country schools of Van Buren County would earn only $30 a month.

Chapter Eleven

THE MARKETS

I N THE EARLY DAYS in Cedar Township, before the railways came in, Fort Madison was the nearest market, other than country stores where butter and eggs could be sold in exchange for groceries and a slim line of drygoods. It was common practice in those days for a farmer to kill and dress his hogs and hang them up to freeze in December or January. When they were frozen solid he would cord the carcasses on a sled and take the load to Fort Madison, and on the return trip bring pine lumber for buildings.

The first country store was called Wilsonville and was located one mile north and a quarter mile west of Tarpleywick. A more important trading center, Hillsboro, was located a mile and one-half south and three and one-half miles east of Tarpleywick, just over the line in Henry County. This had been a post office since 1844, the only one available to Cedar Township settlers until 1872 when a post office was established at Wilsonville. Sometime in the late 1880s Francis Harlan who had been the postmaster at Wilsonville as well as the storekeeper, moved his store to Stockport. At that time the post office was moved to the home of Isaiah Harlan, one mile north and one-half mile east of Tarpleywick, but was discontinued in 1903 when rural free delivery (R.F.D.) was started.

In 1858 the Burlington Railway was extended west from Burlington, Iowa, through Mount Pleasant, Lockridge, and Fairfield. From Tarpleywick the distance was the same to Mount Pleasant, the county seat of Henry County, and to Fairfield, the county seat of Jefferson County. Lockridge was nearer, but there was no bridge across Big Cedar; fording Big Cedar with a wagon was avoided, although cattle were driven from time to time to Lockridge for sale.

Bonapart, located on the Des Moines River eleven miles south of Tarpleywick, became one of the important markets used by Tarpley for the sale of farm products. A letter from the mayor of Bonapart dated February 2, 1967, gives the following information: "In 1857 trains were operating between Keokuk and Bonapart and going as far northwest as Bentonsport. In 1880 the Chicago, Rock Island, and Pacific Railway Co., then the owners of the old K. D. & M. from Keokuk to Des Moines, obtained the roadbed and right of way of the Keokuk, St. Louis, and Missouri. The grade was widened, standard gauge track laid, and that same year the first passenger train was operated into Keosauqua."

To quote further from the mayor, "In the spring of 1837, William Meek, in company with Dr. R. N. Cresap, laid out the town of Bonapart. In 1844 William Meek & Sons built the grist mill and in 1853 the woolen mills. The latter burned in 1863 and were rebuilt by Meek Brothers the same year."

These mills were both operated by waterpower. The Meeks had built a dam across the Des Moines River to provide waterpower for their mills. Bonapart became the most used market and trading place for household supplies, although Fairfield was more favored for buying ready-made clothing and farm implements. Keosauqua, the county seat of Van Buren County, did not become a convenient marketplace for Tarpleywick products. Livestock was taken on the hoof to Bonapart. For cattle this was a relatively simple matter but for hogs ready for the market a walk of eleven miles was no simple matter—either for the hogs or the people taking them. I have a vivid picture in my mind of one trip to Bonapart. I think it was in 1880, with a herd of hogs, fifty or sixty in number. We started about five o'clock in the afternoon. The hogs, which were of the spotted Poland-China breed, were heavier boned and had longer legs than the black Poland-Chinas that became common twenty years later in Iowa. There were four of us in the crew, Tarpley, Sylvanus, one hired man, and me. Sometimes Tarpley would go ahead of the hogs, especially when a bridge was to be crossed. The hogs did not like the sound when their feet

went onto the wooden planks of a bridge, so Tarpley sprin-
kled shelled corn along the approach to the bridge and on
the bridge and led the hogs quietly across. One wagon and
team followed behind. I drove the team. In the wagon was
a supply of oats and hay for the horses, plenty of corn for the
hogs, and some space in which to place a hog in case one
gave out and could not walk the eleven miles. This trip
in the latter part of October was made at night for two reasons, there would be less traffic on the road and it would be
cooler for the hogs. This herd moved along at something
less than a mile an hour on the average and was close to
Bonapart the next morning by six o'clock. Tarpley then
arranged with a farmer for a place to feed and water the
hogs, after which they were taken to the Bonapart stockyards
where they were weighed by the buyer who had in advance
contracted for them at a price. After doing some shopping,
the four of us got in the wagon and returned to Tarpleywick
in about two hours.

There was little marketing of oats and no marketing
of corn and hay from Tarpleywick. Timothy seed, flax seed,
and wool would be taken either to Bonapart, Fairfield, or
Lockridge. During the first twenty years at Tarpleywick
the commercial side of farming became more and more
important; however, the self-sufficient phases of the farm
economy continued to be as important as ever.

In 1882 a narrow-gauge railway was completed from
Fort Madison to a point beyond Cedar Township. The
farmers of the area were very much interested in the promo-
tion of this railway. Tarpley and his brother-in-law each
subscribed $300, and a farmer by the name of McVeigh
offered fifteen acres of land, as well as a money subscription,
if the railway station would be placed on the corner of his
farm just two miles from Tarpleywick. The farmers voted
on the location of the railway station and McVeigh won out.
After that, marketing of livestock and farm products was a
relatively simple matter. A herd of hogs could be driven
to McVeigh in the cool of the morning in about two hours.
A lumberyard and country store were soon established at
McVeigh and this became an important local market for the
remaining years of Tarpley's activities at Tarpleywick, although he still would take the wool clip, timothy seed, and

flax seed to Bonapart or Fairfield, where there were established buyers for these products.

By 1890 McVeigh station was losing its importance. A group of farmers were successful in getting the railway to put in a station and a switch three miles west of Tarpleywick. This new station was named Stockport. A post office was established there on February 27, 1888. This local trading point soon had more than one grocery store, a hardware store, a bank, and two churches. Stockport continued for many years to be the leading local market for the area. With the growth of Stockport, the Wilsonville store dwindled and died.

Chapter Twelve

"IN-SERVICE TRAINING"

A FARM BOY'S TRAINING commences when he is very small and continues to manhood—in fact, as long as he has anything to do with farming. Thus there have always been many people trained in the skills of farming. However, these same people classify as "unskilled" workmen when they desire to enter a city occupation, because agriculture has often been thought of as an "unskilled" occupation. Hence this chapter deals with my "in-service training" and gives a picture of the variety of skills I learned from my father.

My first memory of his training was when I was two years old. He took me with him to the field and had me stand and watch him at work while he was making some repairs on a reaping machine. He always seemed to like to have me with him, even when I was too small to help, and I have no memory of his ever indicating that I was in his way. If he were making a repair at night, he would have me hold the lantern for him and would say, "You hold the lantern so that you can see, then I can see."

I have a clear mental picture of his teaching me to use a small axe, which he had purchased especially for me, when I was six years old. Using very few words, he taught me by example how to swing my little axe and hit the wood I was chopping at exactly the right spot, stroke after stroke, so that the chips flew out of the notch I was cutting with no extra axe marks on them. This required close coordination of hands, arms, and eyes so that the axe hit at exactly the right point with each stroke. It took me quite some time to perfect this skill.

In the garden, he showed me how to use a hoe to destroy weeds and improve the tilth of the soil about the plants without damaging either stalk or roots of the growing plant. When I was a little older, I learned to drive a team. I had to keep my eye ahead on the line of travel and hold the reins so the horses would go in the desired direction. He taught me how to handle a walking plow of the mouldboard type and at the same time control the team that was drawing the plow. During haymaking I turned the grindstone while he sharpened the sickle for the mowing machine. Later, after I had watched many times, he allowed me to try to sharpen the sickle. Throughout the activities of producing and harvesting crops, he carefully taught me the skills of farming.

Machinery of a somewhat complicated character was already in use for planting corn, mowing hay, and reaping small grains and timothy seed. Father always took me with him when he made repairs on this machinery. In 1882, when I was nine years old, my father bought his first self-binding reaping machine. It came to the farm in crates and a man who was supposed to be an expert came and assembled the machine. When my father took it to the field and started to cut oats, everything worked very nicely except the reel turned too fast. It was supposed to turn just fast enough so that each blade of the reel would lay its quota of oats nicely back on the drape which was to carry it to the binder. However, this reel went three or four times too fast and knocked off some of the grain. Since father wanted to cut the oats, he went ahead with the fast reel and sent for the expert. He came and looked everything over, but could not locate the difficulty but promised to report it to the factory. In the meantime, Tarpley arranged to catch the oats the reel batted off and use them for horse feed, hoping the expert would be back with the remedy.

The expert had not yet come back when time came to cut timothy seed. I went with Father when he drove the binder to the timothy field and started cutting. We saw immediately that something had to be done because the fast reel was batting off the timothy seed and it was being lost. Father stopped the machine and together we looked for the cause of the fast reel. I remember how he showed me the

large bull wheel which carried the main load of the machine and was located in the inverted V-shaped space between the drapes that elevate the grain and the binding
mechanism. The bull wheel was also the source of power
for the machine. We noted the gears that activated the shaft
that ran to the back end of the machine. On the end of
this shaft a master sprocket wheel activated a long sprocket
chain that first went over a sprocket wheel for running the
binding mechanism; then to another sprocket wheel operating the elevator drapes; then to a third sprocket wheel driving a shaft that went forward to the reel. The chain then
went to a sprocket wheel activating the drape on the platform of the reaper and delivering the oats to the elevator
drapes. From there it went back to the master sprocket
wheel.

It seemed clear that all these sprocket wheels were of
the right size. However, if the one that sent the power
forward for the reel were greatly increased in size it would
slow down the reel, but we had not studied all of the sprocket
chains.

Father and I went to the front of the machine. Here we
could see the shaft carrying power to the reel. In order that
the reel might be moved up and down, forward and backward, there was an elbow joint equipped with a double
sprocket wheel. One sprocket chain connected the power
shaft to the elbow and another chain carried the power from
the elbow to the reel. I looked at this double sprocket and
noted that the power came in on the small sprocket and
was transmitted by the large sprocket of this double sprocket
wheel. I said to my father, "If you take that double sprocket
wheel off and turn it around so the power will come in on
the larger sprocket wheel and be transmitted by the small
sprocket, that should slow down the reel." Father said
nothing. He took out his pliers, pulled the cotter pin,
loosened the chains, took off the sprocket wheel, reversed
it, put it on the other end, refitted the chains by taking some
links off the upper chain and adding them to the lower
one, and put the cotter pin back in. He was ready to start
the horses and see what would happen. When he got in the
driver's seat and told the horses to move forward, the reel
turned at the proper speed.

Another problem with a self-binding reaping machine
occurred later on. One June day when I was 19 and had

just come home from college, my father said, "I had a lot of trouble with the binder last year, so I think I'll trade it in on a new one." Recalling my early experience with the fast reel, I said, "Let me look it over. Maybe I can put it in shape." My father agreed and added, "The trouble is, it misses binding so many bundles. It will kick out two or three alright, then it will miss one or two. I do not want to enter the harvest with a machine that is not working properly." I took a look at the binding part of the machine and noted that the knotter and other small parts of the binding apparatus were badly worn. I told Father about this and asked where I could get some new parts. He told me that there was a binder of the same make in a field about two miles away which had been used very little. Two farmers had bought the binder together but had quarreled and one of them broke the tongue and otherwise damaged it, and it had been abandoned in the field. However, the moving parts on it were like new. Father arranged for me to get the needed parts from this machine. I went to this binder on horseback, carrying tools in a bag, and got the parts I thought would be needed, including the Appleby knotter.

Father left me entirely to myself in making the repairs. I replaced the worn parts and thought I had solved the problem. But when I went to test the binding equipment, it functioned exactly as Father had said. It would sometimes bind and sometimes miss binding the sheaf.

I was somewhat embarrassed to find that my diagnosis had not been correct. I decided, therefore, to study the operation of the knotter and see if I could find out why it sometimes failed to tie the knot. The knotter had been invented by a man in Wisconsin by the name of Appleby who had watched his grandmother tie a knot on the end of a thread, with one hand. She put the end of the thread between her thumb and two fingers, threw a loop in the thread, and twisted her arm and hand so that the end was pulled through the loop. This observation led him to invent the knotter, and from then on twine was used in binding bundles of grain. Before this invention, wire had been used because the ends could be fastened simply by twisting. But bits of wire sometimes went into the straw pile and in some cases into the cattle that ate the straw, so farmers had hesitated to buy wire binders.

The Appleby knotter was constructed like two fingers

and a thumb. The thumb would rise and let the twine be placed on the fingers by the threaded needle and when the needle withdrew, the thumb would tighten on the thread, the knotter would make a complete turn and tie the "granny knot." It was necessary that the thumb hold the thread tight until the knot was completed. I could see that the difficulty was that the thumb was not holding tightly enough. On examination, I found that the tightness of the thumb depended upon the pressure of a spring at the rear of the knotter. This spring could be adjusted with a screw. When I gave the screw a half turn, the spring held the thumb of the knotter tight to the fingers while the knot was being tied. I then tested the equipment by running a bundle through several times and it bound perfectly every time. I then asked my father to take a look. He was pleased but made no comment. That binder served for three or four more years. This experience taught me to be more careful in my diagnosis.

Father was an excellent teacher. He had led me through all the necessary steps to arrive at the cause of the speedy reel and I was able to apply this method to the repair of the knotter. It was my father's ability to patiently observe and analyze that made Tarpleywick such an excellent place for an apprentice to acquire his "in-service training."

Besides learning skills that required the coordination of hand and eye under the control of the mind, I was also learning how to combine the various crops and livestock enterprises in a manner to provide a relatively even distribution of work throughout the year, and how to avoid allowing the work on one job to seriously conflict with the work on other jobs. In December the butchering was done. Next, wood was cut and hauled to the woodyard. This finished, the sawing and splitting of wood kept us busy for many days. Then there was repairing of fences to be gotten out of the way before work in the fields began. Oats were seeded and then corn was planted. As soon as corn planting was over, sheep shearing was the order of the day. I learned to shear sheep when I was fifteen years of age and took pride in being able to shear as many sheep in a day as my father. By the time sheep shearing was finished, the corn that had been planted first needed to be cultivated.

When I was ten years old, Father taught me how to cultivate corn with a one-row tongueless cultivator drawn by a team of horses. This skill is so important that I shall describe it in detail. He taught me how to run the shovels close to the plants when they were very small so that the row of corn would not become weedy, and how to set the shovels of the cultivator so that they would not destroy the roots of the corn plant when it had grown large and spread its root system. Cultivating close to the corn when it was small was difficult because of the danger of covering the small plants. In order to protect the small corn plants from being covered by soil thrown on them by the forward shovels of the cultivator when they were held adequately close to the corn row, sheet iron fenders about sixteen inches long and six inches wide were fastened to the cultivator beams in such a way that they slid along, edge down, between the shovels and the corn row. This made it possible, when the front shovels were properly set, to cultivate quite close to the corn and rarely cover a plant.

It was a year later before my father sent me to the field with a team and cultivator to work alone. That day, since he was working with a crew repairing a bridge near the corner of the field, he could see how I was getting along. He had furnished me a team that was well trained in cultivating corn; in fact the horses knew more about cultivating corn than I did. All went well. Father had no occasion to come to the field, but we moved very slowly and the number of rows I cultivated that day was not up to standard.

Now that I have given you the picture of corn cultivation as it was done in my youth, we return to the sequence of important seasonal field work. In the latter part of corn cultivation, labor had to be shared with the making of clover hay. Next timothy hay was cut, then came oat harvest, followed by the cutting of timothy for seed, and then threshing. When threshing was over there were a few weeks when nothing was pressing. It was at this time of year in 1880, when I was seven years of age, that my father and mother took me with them to Louisiana, Missouri, where we visited my very aged great-grandmother, as well as various uncles and cousins.

It may seem surprising that after buying so much land in 1879 and so much new machinery in 1880, Tarpley felt financially able to take a vacation in the summer of 1880, but he did, and this trip opened my eyes to a larger world. It remains one of the important landmarks in my life. The steamboat ride down the Mississippi River is the most vivid part of this memory. Someone took the three of us in the carriage, or spring wagon, to Bonapart where we took the train to Keokuk. Thinking that he would give Mother and me a special treat, Father chose to go by river steamboat rather than by train from Keokuk to Louisiana. He made inquiry and was told that the boat would be leaving about six o'clock in the evening and would be in Louisiana in the morning, so we boarded the boat late in the afternoon. I recall that we had frogs' legs for supper, something I had never heard of before. We went to bed in our stateroom expecting to step off the boat in Louisiana in the morning. When morning came we found we were still in Keokuk. It was in the month of August. The water was low in the river. The captain knew there were many sandbars that might cause trouble, so he had waited till morning to start.

In due course, we were moving down the river. Alongside the big side-wheel steamboat was a very large barge loaded with grain which may have slowed down the boat somewhat. We had not been out on the river long before we came to a standstill. The following announcement was soon made, "We have hit a sandbar and must pull through it."

To pull through a sandbar was a slow process. At the front end of the boat there were two large poles, probably sixteen inches in diameter and as much as thirty feet long. The bottom ends of these poles were sharpened so that they could be driven down rather deeply in the sand. The bottom of each pole was placed probably five feet out in front of the boat, then machinery was set in motion that drew the boat up to the poles, and then the poles were set forward again. This process was continued for two or three hours until the boat was pulled over the sandbar. This happened many times on the trip down.

The boat also stopped frequently to load products being shipped south, and every stop seemed to be leisurely. So it was on the third morning, instead of the first morning, that we stepped off at Louisana, Missouri. I have no vivid memory of the return trip, except that we boarded the train in Louisiana and in a few hours were in Keokuk. A few more hours by train and we were back at Bonapart where we were met by someone with the spring wagon.

While we were visiting our relatives we went for a drive on the toll road that ran out of Louisiana. When we stopped at one of the toll gates, I heard my father tell the gatekeeper that he had helped build this road in 1858.

Another memory of that trip relates to the way in which peaches were packed for market. Father's cousin by marriage, Mr. Fry, ran a fruit farm. Apples, peaches, and plums were the principal products. While we were in Louisiana he was marketing peaches. All the members of the family were helping put the peaches in baskets, so I too became a peach packer. Mr. Fry showed me exactly how to put the peaches in the basket. The baskets were so made that the only peaches that showed were in a row on each side at the bottom and a row on each side just under the cover. He told me to pick the finest peaches and fill the sides of the bottom and then put in whatever was available to fill up the basket until close to the top, and the two rows of fine peaches were to be put in, one on each side where they would show, just at the edge of the cover. This was long before the day of uniform grading—it was the day of putting the best food forward. I remembered this little experience when in the Department of Agriculture I became responsible for grading and standardization of fruits and vegetables. My boyhood experience had impressed me with the need for, and the importance of, uniform grading.

After this vacation we came back to many tasks that needed to be done before cornhusking time. Manure had to be hauled and spread, buildings and fences put in good repair. It was important that work of this kind be gotten out of the way before corn picking time, because with 90 acres of corn in the field to be husked out by hand, all available labor was required. It was a very busy time for six weeks or more. This job done, the boys under sixteen or seventeen, including myself, would go to the country school for three months, and my father and the older men who were on the place found many tasks, including cutting of hazel brush on some of the pastureland.

The activities at Tarpleywick provided opportunity for gaining many skills and for getting mental pictures of the way in which a farm needed to be organized and managed in order to be most profitable. The important thing was to keep all the work that could be done *any time* sufficiently caught up so that it did not interfere with the work that had to be done in step with the seasons and the weather: planting, cultivation, and harvesting. For example, if the fences had not been repaired during the winter and the cattle got out during planting or harvesttime, the farmer had to take time to fix fence when he needed to be doing field work. The general rule is: When the crop work is demanding the attention of the farmer, he should "do nothing today that can be put off till a later date," and when work is not pressing "put off nothing that can be done today." The application of this rule requires a good deal of thought. All the things that need to be done have to be kept in mind, big and little. Tarpley was skillful in keeping in mind the great number of little things that had to be done and kept them out of the way of work that had to be done at a specific time of the year.

In-service training extended beyond those living in the household and working on the farm. Commencing in 1880, when father acquired so much additional land, there was usually a family living in the tenast house a quarter mile east of our home. The first of these was John Lazenby, who grew corn and oats on shares, sold the oats that were not needed for his horses, and fed the corn, which he shared, to hogs and poultry. There were about two acres of land that went with the house so the tenant could have a large garden to produce cane for the sorghum mill, and enough to supply his own needs. In those days sorghum molasses was on the farmer's table three times a day. Whenever John Lazenby was not busy with his own crops, he was available to help Tarpley do whatever was to be done. John remained several years and then moved to a farm he had purchased.

Another tenant who occupied the tenant house was Frank Clark. He stayed several years working the land for a share of the crop, raising a good garden, pigs, and chickens, and working for Tarpley when not busy with his own work. In time he too had enough money and bought a farm.

Then, after another tenant, about whom the less said the better, came Elmer Watson with whom Tarpley went into partnership in feeding and caring for sheep. Elmer remained until 1901, then bought a farm. I mention these three tenants, who were really croppers, because what they learned about farming from Tarpley was important in their success as farmers.

Chapter Thirteen

TARPLEY EARLY TAYLOR

M Y FATHER, Tarpley Early Taylor, 1837–1904, was
of the seventh generation of the Taylor line in
America, the ninth generation of the Tarpley line,
and the fifth generation of the Early line. This resulted in
his combining elements of three nationalities. Scottish blood
dominated, German was next in importance, and English
accounted for about one-sixteenth.

He was about five feet ten inches tall, well-muscled, and
lean. His hair was black, but his full beard was dark red.
When he died at sixty-seven years of age he showed signs of
gray hair but no baldness. Tarpley's eyes—deep set and very
expressive—were the center of interest in his face. He was
not a talkative person, but one could tell by looking him in
the eye that he was thinking seriously of whatever subject
was under consideration even when he did not speak. At
such times he would sometimes turn his head a little to one
side and slightly open his lips as if he were going to speak,
and then say nothing. To me this always meant that he
had decided to make no comment, and I always felt free to
proceed with the program I had presented to him. At the
dining table or in the living room when there was company,
he seldom had much to say either.

He had a sense of humor but usually kept it to himself.
However, on one occasion he told me that during the Civil
War, when the army was buying horses for the cavalry, he
sold his last horse to the army purchasing agent and his
father said to him, "Now, Tarpley, how are you going to
operate your farm?" Tarpley knew that he could buy horses

Tarpley of Tarpleywick

The church in Stockport

in the area, not suitable for the army, that would serve his purpose on the farm at a price much lower than the one he had received. Instead of saying this to his father, he said, "I have a very large hoe." Tarpley had a big smile on his face when he told me this story.

He was not a gossip and never talked about his neighbors in a critical or jocular mood. He also ignored jibes aimed at him. When he was taking the lead in building the church at Stockport, some of the neighbors spoke of the church building as "Tarpley's sheep shed." He certainly knew what they were saying but he made no response. He took advantage of the fact that people knew he was hard of hearing and that they did not know whether or not he had heard what had been said, although he often did. While he was a silent man, he was never moody or sullen and never carried a grudge. He was the first in the neighborhood to buy new laborsaving machinery. One of his neighbors who had seven sons called these machines "a lazy man's equipment." When this was repeated to Tarpley he said nothing.

Tarpley had plenty of confidence in his ability to accomplish anything he undertook. He was highly persistent in carrying out his undertakings, whether it was work on the farm or in the community. He felt if a thing needed to be done he could find a way to do it, and it was remarkable how generally those associated with him fell in line to perform the necessary tasks. His leadership provided inspiration for those who followed. And if there were others who conspired to defeat him by blocking the way, he found some other route of accomplishing his purpose, but did not fight.

In the early spring of 1879 eighty acres of land a half mile west of the Tarpleywick residence was for sale at public auction to settle an estate. The advertisement stated that the forty acres north of the road would be put up for sale, then the forty acres with the farm buildings south of the road would be offered for sale. This done, both forties would be offered as a unit.

When the forty north of the road was offered by the auctioneer there were no bids, and when the forty south of the road was offered there were no bids. Then the whole farm was put on the auction block and Tarpley bid it off at a very reasonable price. Some of those present felt he was getting it too cheap. They put their heads together and asked the auctioneer to repeat the offer by forties and the two forties were bid off at a price slightly higher than Tarpley's bid for the whole. Of course the latter move was illegal. According to the rules of the auction Tarpley had acquired the land, but for reasons of his own he withdrew from the auction and left the land in the hands of those who had only intended to force up his bid.

In later years, when I heard of this, I asked him why he did not insist on his rights at that auction, and he replied, "I just decided to expand my farm toward the east rather than toward the west." Before the end of that year he had acquired 180 acres of land immediately adjacent to land which he held in sections 15, 16, and 22, and it made a much more manageable farm than would have been possible by expansion to the west.

This freedom of choice in buying land was possible at that time because many people were leaving Iowa to take up holdings under the Homestead Act which gave a bona fide settler 160 acres of land at no cost beyond a filing fee, construction of a minimum of farm buildings, and some land cultivation. As already noted in Chapter 3, the land Tarpley bought in 1879 was in four separate pieces, each of which had been a separate farm. There were four sets of buildings and four orchards. These farmers had seized the opportunity to greatly improve their financial condition by selling their little farms at a price that was attractive to my father and by then going west to take up a homestead.

For a man busy operating a 500-acre farm, father managed to do a great deal of reading, especially in the wintertime when the days were short and the evenings long. He read the Bible more than any other book, but he also had several books on agriculture which were well worn from use. Information such as is now available to the farmer about breeding, feeding, and care of stock, about the choice of seeds, and about the market outlook for his products was not available. A farmer had to depend largely on his own experience and the experience of his neighbors.

During my years on the farm, working under my father's supervision, he never praised me, either for the quantity or the quality of my work. I never heard him praise anyone; on the other hand he was not critical either. On one occasion, on the second of July when I was fifteen years of age, he said to me, "I want you to give a final cultivation to that ten acres of corn planted late because of wet weather. The rest of us will be working in the hay." I asked for the team of 1,100-pound mares, Kate and Flora. I knew they could walk along briskly with the "New Departure" tongue-less cultivator because the soil was loose, not having been beaten down by heavy rain. By 11:30, when the dinner bell rang, I had cultivated more than a third of the ten-acre field, and believed I could finish the field in the afternoon, with a fresh team. At noon I asked for the mule team, Jack and Jim, and hurried back to the field after dinner. The well-trained team shuttled back and forth on the corn rows, turning from one row to the next, and at six o'clock I drove into the barnyard with the cultivator. Father said, "What's the matter? Did you break something?" I replied, "Nothing's broken. I finished the job!" Father said nothing. However, I knew that I had set a record—no one in the area had ever before cultivated ten acres of corn in one day.

The next morning at breakfast he said, "We will start the mower this morning on that field where there is very little clover in the timothy and we can put it up this afternoon." This was a shift in his plans. He had planned to put up the hay that had already been cut down and knock off at noon, since it was the day before the holiday. He had expected me to finish the corn cultivation at that time. He did not explain why he made this change and all hands worked with the hay all day. My cultivating the ten acres

of corn in one day with a one-row cultivator may have given
him the impulse that produced the change in plan. The
next day, on the way to the celebration which was held in
Farmer McVeigh's maple grove, we passed the ten-acre field.
My father kept glancing down the corn rows as we drove
along, but he didn't say anything.

Another time when my accomplishment appeared to
influence his thinking was in 1896. I had prepared the land
and planted 65 acres of oats and 100 acres of corn with the
help of a boy and two three-horse teams and had given the
whole corn area its third cultivation within a period of ten
days without any help. At this time he remarked, "I have
decided to be very careful in selecting men to work the
land in order to get the job done with fewer men."

Tarpley attended church regularly. Each Sunday morning he would have breakfast and take care of the livestock
as on other mornings. Then he would hitch the team to
the spring wagon and drive around to the hitching post along
the road west of the house. Beside the hitching post there
was a little platform just the right height to allow the
family to step from the yard into the spring wagon without
having to climb up. He would tie the team to the post and,
if the weather were cold, would blanket the horses. Then he
went into the house, washed up, and put on his Sunday
clothes. By this time Elmira had seen to it that the children
were dressed for church and by 9:30 everyone was in the
spring wagon and on the way.

Sunday School began at ten o'clock and was followed by
the church service. About once a month an itinerant preacher
would lead the service and preach. On other Sundays one
of the farmers of the community, many of whom were regular readers of the Bible, would lead the service. Tarpley
took his turn as leader of the Sunday service.

There was religious activity in the home as well as in
the church. At the beginning of every meal the blessing was
asked. Each evening before going to bed the family would
sit down in a circle while Tarpley read a chapter from the
Bible; then we would all kneel in prayer, with Tarpley voic-
ing the prayer.

There was no feeling on the part of the members of the
family that we were required to go to Sunday School and
church or that we were required to participate in the eve-

ning religious service in the home. We accepted this plan of life as the natural thing to do. Occasionally if one member desired to stay home on Sunday, he was allowed to do so. And if someone slipped off to bed before evening prayer, nothing was said, but this rarely happened.

It was common practice, when a visitor was at our table, for Tarpley to ask the guest to pronounce the blessing. One such occasion was when Jake Rockey, who had a forty-acre farm three-quarters of a mile east of Tarpleywick, was helping father with the hay. Jake was a great talker and his language contained a good many biblical words used very freely! How much of this Tarpley heard will never be known. At half past eleven, the dinner bell rang and the crew working in the hay went to the house. When we were seated at the dining table Tarpley turned to Jake and asked him to offer the blessing. Jake rose to the occasion and did a respectable job. That afternoon in the field he was a silent man.

Tarpley was a very earnest person, interested first of all in his family, and devoting the major part of his energy to making a success of farming. But he was always interested in the local church, and in mission work at home and abroad.

Tarpley's religious activities went hand in hand with his interest in the farm and the family. He served as church treasurer and always headed the annual subscription for supporting the local church with a larger sum than anyone else was expected to give. When the town of Stockport was started, he took the lead in the financial risks in building a church there, but continued to help support the old neighborhood church a mile and a quarter north and east of Tarpleywick. He was much interested in church extension work in Iowa and worked with the State Secretary in raising a $100,000 fund for investment, the income of which was to pay the salary and expenses of the State Secretary so that none of the funds later raised by the Church Secretary would need to be used for the Secretary's salary and expenses. About the last local undertaking in which Tarpley was active was the raising of a fund to buy additional land to enlarge the cemetery. An endowment fund was also set up for maintaining the cemetery.

The general attitude of Tarpley toward work and life is illustrated by a short story I wrote in 1930 when I was thinking about my father's religious interests, the way they affected his financial interests, and the way they affected his relations to those who worked with him on the farm. The story which follows, put in fiction form with respect to names, was close enough to the things that happened on the farm and at the local church that my oldest sister Laura could name all the characters that had been fictionalized. The story reads as follows:

Advancing the Cause

A farmer by the name of Martin once lived on the edge of the woods by the side of the prairie. Through industry and thrift he acquired much land, some of which he let to tenants who worked it for a share of the crops. As he was driving over his land one day, accompanied by the community preacher, he stretched the whip out over the land with a gesture indicating its scope and said, "I look upon it as my duty to handle this land in such a manner as will best advance the Cause." In their language "the Cause" meant just one thing—the advancement of Christianity. The preacher was delighted, for to him this meant, first of all, larger subscriptions for the local church and for missions. The preacher pointed out various ways whereby the farmer could extract more out of his tenants and thus better serve "the Cause." After listening patiently for a time, the farmer said, "But I do not want to take more from these men. I want them to prosper, buy farms in this community, and be themselves supporters of "the Cause."

Twenty years later, when Farmer Martin had gone to his reward, the preacher returned after a long absence to the old church to help celebrate the dedication of a fine new church building, fully equipped to serve the needs of a rural religious and social center. The prosperous farmer who met him at the train in a powerful car had been a tenant on Martin's land twenty years before. He had since acquired a farm of his own and become the leader who had promoted the new church building. As they drove to this farmer's home, talking of the past and of the present important work of building a better community, the preacher recalled Farmer Martin's words of twenty years before and recognized their wisdom.

From 1860 to 1880 Father's major attention had been given to expanding the area of Tarpleywick. After that he had more time for community activities. For as long as I can remember, he was a member of the Grange. When I started to country school, I saw a large corner cupboard to the right of the entrance door and was told that that was

where the Grangers kept their "goat." Later, when one of
the Grangers came during the noon recess and opened the
cupboard, there was no goat! It was obvious that the cupboard was for all kinds of things used by the Grange at its
meetings which were held in the schoolhouse.

The most outstanding activity of the Grange while I
was growing up on the farm was the Grange Fair and Picnic
held forty rods east of the center of Cedar Township in the
Tarpleywick wooded pasture. This started off as little more
than a picnic but it grew to such proportions that the offi-
cials of the County Fair complained that the Grange Fair
was damaging the County Fair. Cedar Township was in the
northeast corner of Van Buren County, and the Grange Fair
drew crowds from all over the northeast third of the county.

In preparation for this fair, a speakers' stand was put
up and seats were made by placing eight-inch planks on
stringers made of logs. There were stalls for horses and
pens for cattle, sheep, and hogs. Finally, a Fine Arts Building was constructed. Here the ladies exhibited all kinds of
fancywork, products of the kitchen, and homemade dresses.
For many, many years only ribbons were given as prizes,
and everybody seemed satisfied.

On the day of the fair, a string of horsedrawn vehicles
forty rods long lined up for their turn at the ticket office
outside the gate at the entrance to the fairgrounds. The
first sound one heard as one entered was the martial music.
An old soldier named Sneath dressed in blue played the
flute. Orr Davidson beat the bass drum, and Bert Davidson
played the tenor drum. On one occasion I remember there
was also a brass band. Another old soldier, Ross Wheatley,
was astride a fine horse and decorated with a red sash.
Wheatley, as marshall of the day, was to keep order and make
sure that only legitimate soft drinks were sold at the vending
counters set up for the occasion by merchants from all the
nearby towns. As the guest of the fair went about the grounds
viewing all of the exhibits and visiting with the people he
met, he not only learned about what his neighbors were
doing on the farm and in the home, but he stopped and
visited with his friends and made new acquaintances.

One big event not to be lost sight of in recalling the
scene was the midday picnic when the people set out the
contents of their baskets on red and white tablecloths spread

on the closely grazed bluegrass. Families and friends joined together in groups, and these picnicking groups could be seen scattered over many acres of the woodland pasture. Some of those present had come to the McVeigh railway station by train from both east and west, and the management of the fair had arranged to have farm wagons with spring seats at the station to bring them to the fair. This was an occasion when many young men brought their best girls for an outing, and where some of them met for the first time the young women who became their wives.

In the afternoon the guests at the fair gathered on the seats in front of the speakers' stand and listened to addresses made by the congressmen of the area, the county school superintendent, and other available speakers.

The fair lasted only one day but those who set up their stands and brought their livestock came the day before to prepare, and many of them remained till the next morning. Then the young boys of the neighborhood went carefully over the areas where business had been transacted, looking for any coins that might have been lost. This is the picture that I hold in mind after seventy-five years.

My father gave special attention to getting the members of his family established in life. I recall that in the spring of 1883 my older brother married Carrie Morris. As mentioned before, the two families were close friends. My father gave Sylvanus the ninety-acre farm in section 10 which had been acquired when Grandfather Martin's estate was settled. This land had not been incorporated into Tarpleywick but left as a separate unit. It had a good house and barn. Father also provided Sylvanus with a team and wagon and the necessary farm equipment.

The following year my oldest sister Laura married a farmer and my father helped them buy a farm. About two years later my sister Lou said she wanted to go to college and Tarpley agreed to help her as much in going to college as he had helped Laura in buying a farm. It was then that I knew I could have my choice, land for a farm or money for schooling.

I had started school in 1878, when I was five years old, and went to school in the wintertime as late as 1890. The most outstanding teacher during the years I attended the country school was Edgar Harlan, who later became curator of the Iowa Historical Collections in Des Moines. He taught the school when I was twelve years of age. I do not recall all the subjects I was studying, but I do vividly recall that arithmetic and history were the outstanding subjects. About a month before the closing of the term, Ed came to my desk and noticed that I was working examples in arithmetic many pages ahead of the class. He said, "That is fine. Keep on and you will be able to write *Ne Plus Ultra* on the back page of the book by the end of the term." In our history we had read that before the days of Columbus someone had written on the east side of Gibraltar, these three Latin words. This impressed me very much. A few days before the end of the term Ed came to my desk and saw that I was working on the last page of Ray's Third Part. He stooped over and said, "Don't write *Ne Plus Ultra,* write *Plus Ultra.* There is much beyond as you will discover." This made an indelible impression upon my mind—and now as I am just ready to commence my ninety-fifth year, *Plus Ultra* is leading me on.

The Literary Societies in the schools of the area provided the forum in which I got my early experience as a public speaker. I have no very pleasant memories of the spelling matches, but the debating matches I can look back upon with delight. I continued to debate in at least four of the school-houses in Cedar Township as late as the winter of 1894–1895, when I taught the Taylor school.

So far as my accomplishments in the country school are concerned, I have only this measure. I went to the Drake preparatory department in 1891, and five years later I was graduated with a bachelor's degree from the Iowa State College at Ames.

Beginning in 1891 my father financed my schooling for the next ten years, during which time, however, a fellowship and some earnings helped pay the bills. In all the years from the time I started to college in 1891 until I returned from my student days in Europe, Father never said a word to encourage or discourage me. But whenever I asked for funds they were available.

There was one exception to his traditional silence with regard to my plans. Upon returning from Europe in 1901, I went directly home. One day Father and I were repairing a fence on the piece of land he had bought that year. I liked the farm, and while working alongside Tarpley I had that warm feeling I always had when working with him, and I said, "Now, after ten years I have the education that I had hoped to get in a year or two. I feel that I would be very happy running this farm." Tarpley spoke up quickly, "You are well prepared for far more important work, and there are plenty of people to run farms."

When the postman came that afternoon he brought a letter from the University of Wisconsin offering me a job. Two years after I took my first position at the University of Wisconsin, he came to visit me. He had a private conference with Professor Richard T. Ely and Professor Scott, but never told me anything that had been said in these conferences. The same thing had been true of a letter that Professor Ely had written to him in 1897, when I had been making my decision to continue my education with a view to participating in the development of agricultural economics in the United States. Tarpley never told me a single word that was in the letter.

After he had had the conferences with Professor Ely and Professor Scott in the forenoon, instead of going to my boardinghouse for our midday meal, we went downtown to the Simons Hotel. After dinner he asked about furniture stores. That afternoon he went shopping and bought me a very comfortable morris chair. "I think," he said, "you should have a better chair than the one furnished you."

Chapter Fourteen

ELMIRA MARTIN TAYLOR

M Y MOTHER was of average height and had friendly brown eyes and wavy auburn hair. She had a warmer personality than my father and she talked more. Her interest centered on her home and her family. From the time she was a bride she not only made a comfortable home for my father but the work she did was an essential part of the farm economy. The extent of her contribution, just in processing food, was very large. The picture of the farmhouse cellar brimming with food preserved for the winter was impressive, but if to that we could add the baking and cooking that went on every day of the year, it would be staggering. After she moved into the frame house in 1866, she had a loom in the smokehouse. Incidentally this loom had been made by her father. On it she wove cloth for clothing and rag rugs for the floors. The poultry, of course, required care the year round and provided eggs and meat for the table as well as eggs for trading at the store. Furthermore, there was a flock of geese, and every spring their breasts were plucked for making new feather beds and pillows.

Most important of all there were the children. Sylvanus and Laura have already been mentioned. A second daughter was born January 19, 1869. She was named Anna Louella, but always called Lou. On April 16, 1873, I was born. My Grandfather Taylor took great pride in announcing to one and and all that I was the first red-haired Taylor in 200 years.

My mother's knowledge of folk medicine has already

been mentioned. Besides the lore she had learned from her mother she studied a large yellow leather-bound medical book which had a conspicuous place in the kitchen. One example will suffice to illustrate her skill with healing herbs and roots. When I was just a little fellow, I had gone to town with my father and was waiting in the wagon for him to do an errand. The team became frightened and started up, upsetting the wagon and throwing me to the ground so that my left leg was pinned under the heavy wagon box. Luckily the horses stopped when I shouted, "Whoa!" But my thigh was injured so that there was an open sore three inches long and more than an inch wide. Mother watched this sore carefully and when she saw that there was danger of gangrene she sent someone to dig up a burdock root. She sliced this root and fried it in lard. The ointment that resulted was applied freely to the injury. My leg soon healed.

These were the days when families cared for their injured and sick and aged at home. Sometime during the summer of 1876 my uncle John Pleasant Taylor became ill and father brought him and his four children to Tarpley-wick. John Pleasant's wife had died about two years earlier, and until he became ill he had been able to care for his family in his own home with the help of a housekeeper. However, when he fell ill he needed more care than he could be given in his own home.

Father and Mother had been thinking of enlarging their house so when John Pleasant and his four children came, the remodeling was started immediately. The upper floor of the house was changed to a dormitory for the four girls and another for the four boys; there was also a bedroom up there for Father and Mother. In the meantime, the smokehouse was used as a kitchen and the room that had been the kitchen was turned into a room for John Pleasant.

When our cousins came to live with us, Sylvanus was almost fourteen years old and John Pleasant's oldest child William was thirteen; Laura was ten, the same age as John Pleasant's oldest daughter Anna; Lou was seven and John Pleasant's second daughter Elizabeth was about a year older; I was three and John Pleasant's second son George was five. John Pleasant died on the fourth of September, 1876. On his deathbed he begged Tarpley and Elmira to take his four children into their family. This gave mother a difficult problem. The John Pleasant children had been without a mother for more than two years and had received less than normal discipline.

Mother found herself in charge of the "in-service training" of four girls. The first principle she adopted was that of equal treatment of Laura and Anna with respect to work and discipline. She showed no special favors to her daughter Laura. The same principles applied to the two younger girls who were old enough to perform some household tasks. At first this plan was not highly acceptable to the newcomers because they looked upon themselves as guests in the house, but gradually they became part of the family.

William worked with Sylvanus in carrying on the farm work and had the benefit of the "in-service training" Tarpley was so competent in providing. When William had received as much education as he could get at the country school, he went to Whittier Academy in Salem, Iowa, and soon had a teacher's certificate in Van Buren County. Anna and Elizabeth were also provided with funds from their father's estate for some schooling away from home and all three eventually became country school teachers; however, they continued to look upon Tarpleywick as home.

William married one of the Morris girls when he was nineteen and received his share of his father's estate. He went to Nebraska, where in due course he owned an 1,100-acre farm in Custer County. For about twenty-five years he was a member of the state legislature. Anna married Bert Campbell, a farmer in the neighborhood where she taught school. She used her share of her father's estate to help her husband buy a farm. Elizabeth went to Nebraska, taught country school, and married George Baumann, a competent farmer. George, the youngest, began to suffer from tuberculosis of the bone before he was twelve years of age. After two serious illnesses, during which he was cared for at Tarpleywick, he was laid to rest beside his parents in the Hillsboro cemetery. And thus ended the service that John Pleasant had asked of my father and mother.

My Grandfather Martin lived at Tarpleywick during the last years of his life, and after being an invalid for about a year, died in 1881. That same year my youngest sister Carrie was born. But some of the children were already grown. In the preceding chapter the marriage of Sylvanus in 1883 and of Laura in 1884 have already been mentioned. So the family which had been so numerous was reduced to five: Father and Mother, Lou, fifteen years old, Carrie, three years old, and myself, eleven.

The years from 1876 to 1884 had been extremely busy ones for my mother. In addition to the ordinary household duties there had been the care of four orphaned children, four extended periods of providing hospital care for the sick, three funerals, the birth of another daughter, two "infares" when William and Sylvanus brought home their brides, and two weddings, one for Laura and one for Anna.

It was the custom in Cedar Township in the 1880s for the wedding to take place in the home of the bride at about midday, and after the ceremony all of the party was served a sumptuous dinner. The bride and groom remained at the home of the bride until the next morning. About midforenoon the bride and groom, parents, brothers and sisters, and other close kin of the bride drove over to the home of the groom. There, another great feast was served, and besides the bride's kin, the close kin of the groom were invited. This was called the "infare." That evening after dark, the men and boys of the surrounding neighborhood gathered around the house of the groom's parents for the "shivaree." They brought all kinds of equipment for making noise, cowbells, shotguns loaded only with powder, or just boards that could be clapped together—anything to make a noise. This crowd cheered and made all kinds of noise, until the groom, accompanied by the bride, stepped out of the house to greet them. The groom usually had a box of cigars in his hand. At the appearance of the bride and groom everyone became silent and after the cigars had been passed around the "shivaree" party dispersed.

The eight strenuous years had taken their toll and Elmira's beautiful auburn hair was streaked with gray. During the years that followed, Elmira's responsibilities were comparatively light. In 1887 Lou entered Drake University in Des Moines and four years later I too went there to study. When Carrie was ready for high school she began her studies in Kansas City, Kansas, where Lou was teaching, and later continued them at Drake until she was called home by Mother's death.

My mother died February 21, 1901, when she was just

Elmira of Tarpleywick

Henry C. Taylor with his sisters Carrie (left) and Lou.

past fifty-eight years of age. But the influence of her life continues. At the time of her death, I was in London doing research in the Library of the British Museum, and attending lectures at the London School of Economics. One evening I returned to my room and found two letters from home. One was from my mother and all was going well. The other was from my oldest sister Laura telling of Mother's death. This was the most devastating news I had ever received. I was so shocked that my work became ineffective. The two years I had planned to spend abroad were almost over, so I began to plan my return home. During this period I wrote to a very dear friend, an American I had met at a German university where we were fellow students. I told him of the great misfortune that had overtaken me. He was a student of religion and was studying the new interpretations of the Bible which were being unfolded by the German theologians. I found great solace in the letter he wrote me. He had lost both his father and mother before coming to Germany and could speak in the light of his own experience. He said, "At first, after such a loss as you have sustained, death will have seemed to end all. But in time your day of Pentecost will come and you will realize that the spirit of your mother is still with you, built into your life permanently. Then the pain will cease and thankfulness for what your mother has meant to you will give you peace and guide your life." This proved to be true and until this day when any vital moral issue must be settled, I feel that the spirit of my mother is present to guide me.

It seems as though it were only yesterday that she was alive. I see her sitting in a pew, well forward in the church, with her head thrown back, singing with her rich soprano voice. I see her busily engaged in household duties. My last vision of her was standing on the grass west of the Tarpley-wick house in July 1899, as she was smilingly waving good-bye to me as Father and I drove away toward the railway station. I was starting my trip to Europe for further prepara-tion for my lifework.

The relationship of my father and mother was quiet and peaceable. I never heard them quarrel about anything. They were partners in the important business of raising a family. Their equal involvement is illustrated by the follow-ing: When I was away from home, Mother wrote a letter to me every week. This had been the custom for ten years. When she died, Father immediately took up the pen where she had laid it down and wrote to me each week. Of course I wrote equally often. The harmony between them was just one of many happy things in their relationship. However, they were not openly affectionate toward each other in the presence of their children.

Now almost sixty-eight years after the death of my mother and sixty-four years after the death of my father, I often reflect upon the home life at Tarpleywick and the way in which it influenced my life. Mother and Father stand out in my memory, and I feel sure that without what they did for me in giving me a healthy start in life, high ideals, and an excellent preparation, I could never have made as good a record as that which is behind me. So to them belongs the credit for what I have accomplished. I loved my mother and held my father in high esteem.

Chapter Fifteen

THE RUBYS ❖ 1901–1916

TARPLEY and his youngest daughter, Carrie Sabelle, had managed to get along at Tarpleywick during the spring and summer of 1901. In order that Carrie might continue her schooling and Tarpley might be relieved of the responsibility of operating the farm, Laura, Tarpley's oldest daughter, and her husband John W. Ruby, moved to Tarpleywick and disposed of their ninety-acre farm a mile and a half north of Tarpleywick. John took over the management of the farm, and Laura took charge of the household and made a home for Tarpley.

Even though the Rubys were at Tarpleywick, Carrie and I, the only unmarried members of the family, continued to think of Tarpleywick as home, although we were there only on vacations.

The household continued to be operated much the same as it had been in previous years. The poultry yard yielded hundreds of dozens of eggs and a great supply of fryers. The garden and truck patch and the orchards made the same contributions toward the family living as in earlier years.

In a letter from Gladys Carolyn Ruby, dated January 30, 1967, she writes: "One of my most vivid impressions of farm life at the beginning of the twentieth century was the fact that our family was almost self-sufficient in the production of food supplies. In addition to meat, eggs, and dairy products, we always had an abundance of fruits and vegetables which were stored for winter use. The more perishable fruits and vegetables were either canned or dried for

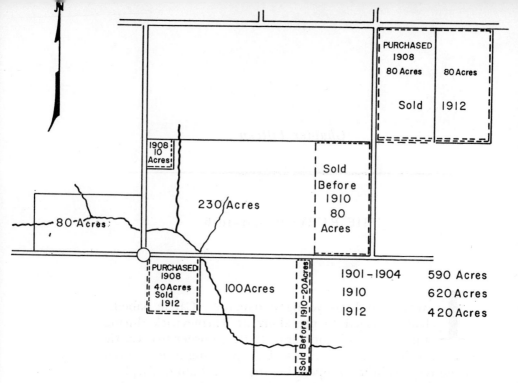

The Rubys at Tarpleywick (land sold)

storage. Others, such as apples, potatoes, celery, cabbage, turnips, parsnips, etc., were stored in the basement. All left-over cider was kept for vinegar. As long as Grandfather was able, he kept us well supplied with delicious clover honey. Refrigeration was provided during the summer through the use of ice which was cut from the farm pond and packed in sawdust for later use."

When the Rubys took over the management of Tarpley-wick, it contained 590 acres of land, and was well stocked with cattle, horses, sheep, and hogs. When John Ruby sold his farm he brought his livestock and equipment to supplement those already on the farm. Until the autumn of 1904, the Rubys operated the farm on a tenancy basis, but in 1904, a few days before his death, Tarpley deeded 390 acres of the land to John W. and Laura T. Ruby (with obligations to other members of the family to equalize the distribution of his estate). At the same time he deeded 100 acres each to his daughters Louella T. Hastings and Carrie Sabelle Taylor. This made no change in the operation of Tarpleywick. The Rubys farmed, on a tenancy basis, the land which had been deeded to Louella and to Carrie, and in due course acquired the 100 acres that had been deeded to Carrie Sabelle Taylor. In 1909 they acquired the 10 acres in the northwest corner of the southwest quarter of section 15 which had been in possession of Tarpley's brother, William Allen Taylor, until his death October 27, 1908. They also acquired the northwest quarter of the northwest quarter of section 22, a very handy piece of land of excellent quality, just across the road from the south side of Tarpleywick barn lot, and the west half of the northwest quarter of section 14. But about the same time 100 acres consisting of the east half of the southeast quarter of section 15 and the east quarter of the west half of the northeast quarter of section 22, which he had leased from Louella Taylor Hastings, were sold by Louella and withdrawn from the Tarpleywick operation. By 1910 Tarpleywick consisted of 620 acres. However, in 1912 the 160 acres in section 14 and the 40 acres in the northwest quarter of section 22 were sold, reducing the farm to 420 acres.

When John Ruby and his two boys, Boyd and Taylor Ruby, took over the operation of the farm in the autumn of 1901, Boyd was fourteen years of age and Taylor was twelve. No radical changes were made in the farming at Tarpleywick when the Rubys took over. Cattle, horses, sheep, and hogs continued to be kept in about the same proportions as in Tarpley's day. Corn, oats, clover, and timothy for hay or for seed continued to be the principal crops.

The management and the day-to-day operation of the farm were planned by the group-thinking methods in which all members of the family participated. I was told that in these farm-planning conferences John and Boyd discussed matters rather freely while Taylor sat and thought. Finally John would say, "Taylor, what do you think about it?" Taylor would sum up the results of the conversation and his thinking, stating what he thought should be done. John would say, "That's what we'll do." It was said that Taylor talked often with his grandfather Tarpley and thus drew upon Tarpley's forty years of experience at Tarpleywick.

In speaking of this early period of the Rubys at Tarpleywick, in a letter dated February 10, 1967, Taylor Early Ruby wrote, "Grandfather took very little active part in anything pertaining to the operation of the farm. He retained a very fine looking, high life, black horse and a one-horse buggy. He gave much care and attention to this horse which he drove, hitched to the buggy, for his transportation. During good weather he spent much time, as I recall, making trips to Stockport, reconstructing a house adjacent to the Christian Church. It was to be for the use of the minister. I am inclined to think that he paid for the total cost of the lot and the house. I recall helping him some with the reconstruction work and the painting of the parsonage property."

During the Ruby period of operation, commencing in the autumn of 1901 and ending in the autumn of 1912, the land was well cared for. There was some improvement in the crop production and quality of livestock. The latter was especially marked in the quality of the shorthorn cattle. In Tarpley's day the English type of shorthorn had been kept, but the Rubys switched to the Scottish type which made better beef but produced less milk.

Quoting further from a letter from Taylor Early Ruby dated February 10, 1967:

When Father and Mother moved over to Grandfather's place during the fall of 1901, both Boyd and I were old enough to handle a team and do farm work. I still recall that it seemed to be a never-ending task, feeding the livestock, milking and taking care of the stock in a variety of ways, as well as looking after the buildings and fences. I do not recall having any dislike in doing what needed to be done since it appeared to me that there was considerable importance to what we were doing and that there was a real measure of achievement.

As a report on Father and Mother's activity pertaining to operating this land, I would like to make the following comments as to what they accomplished. Both Boyd and I started to school at Drake in the fall of 1904. However, during three of the four years that I was at Drake, two preparing for college and two for my college work, I went home during the spring and summer terms to help out with the farm work. These years kept me in touch with much of father's activity on the farm.

Father practiced crop rotation very consistently, raised cattle, hogs, sheep, and colts, and did considerable cattle, hog, and sheep feeding. He returned all the manure from the barns and lots to the areas of the land which needed it most and I was able to see the favorable results in better production.

Aside from crop work, I helped with all other types of work, such as dehorning cattle, castrating pigs, calves, lambs, and colts, marking the sheep, calves, and pigs, and the cutting off of the tails of the lambs. We usually hired the sheep sheared of their wool since this work came when we were very busy in the fields during the planting season for the crops.

There was always a certain amount of time required looking after the livestock when they were in pasture, providing them with salt, checking their condition, and making sure there was an adequate supply of water, and that the fences were in good repair.

After the spring planting season and corn cultivation, there was the task of putting up great quantities of hay, the cutting and threshing of oats, barley, wheat, and timothy and clover for seed. Then followed the picking of the corn crop.

As a result of all this activity and effort on the farm, Father was able to market yearly about two carloads of fat cattle, two or more carloads of fat hogs, and approximately two carloads of sheep, considerable wool, several grown horses, considerable timothy and clover seed, and some milk or cream. All other major crops were used for feed. On several occasions I went to Chicago along with carload shipments of stock.

Aside from this stated marketing of crops, we raised a great portion of our food requirements, beef, pork, lard, mutton, chickens, butter, milk, eggs, apples, pears, peaches, grapes, potatoes, tomatoes, celery, cabbage, etc. It was a subsistence type of living. It was a good and constructive type of life. One got a good return for plans and efforts. I like to think that the purpose, direction, and effort which Grandfather and Grandmother and my father and mother, and others of their family established have enabled succeeding generations to make a contribution to society, rather than being a burden to progress.

During much of the period John Ruby was at Tarpleywick, he and my brother Sylvanus E. Taylor owned and operated the best threshing outfit in that area. It consisted of a steam engine of the tractor type, a grain separator, a clover huller, and an excellent outfit for sawing stove wood. This equipment was used not only for doing their own threshing and wood cutting but also for doing custom work.

The Rubys not only acquired additional land, but also educated their family. By 1910 Boyd and Taylor had both graduated from college and the oldest daughter, Gladys Carolyn, was well along in her college course. While at Tarpleywick, the family was also increased by two additional daughters, Helen Elmira, born December 19, 1903, and Laura Kathryn, born June 20, 1909.

It was sometime in 1912 that I received a letter from my sister Laura telling me that they were going to move to Des Moines. I had been warned a year or two earlier that this might happen. The family had bought a Buick automobile and I had said to my sister, "You could have modernized your house for what that automobile cost." She had responded, "When we leave, we can take the automobile with us, but we will leave the house behind." Hence, I was not completely surprised.

Thus in 1912 the period of the direct operation of Tarpleywick by John W. Ruby and his family was terminated.

Prior to moving to Des Moines in the autumn of 1912 John and Laura Ruby leased Tarpleywick to Boyd and Alta Miller. In advance of doing so, John had sold his usual quota of cattle, horses, sheep, and hogs. The remainder of the livestock and most if not all of the machinery, certainly not including the threshing machine, were included in the crop and livestock share lease, and Miller paid, or agreed to pay, for a half interest in the livestock. The custom would have been for Miller to buy outright such machinery and tools as he took over from Ruby. Under this contract the gross income, minus such expenses as Ruby and Miller had agreed to share, was divided equally.

This change of occupancy of Tarpleywick did not mean that the farm had gone completely out of the family. The Rubys still owned the farm, and Alta Wheatly Miller was a niece of Tarpley's. Hence, the life in the home and the operation of the farm went on for the next four years much as it had in the Ruby period.

In the autumn of 1916 the Boyd Miller tenancy was brought to a close and the joint property sold at public auction. This ended the operation of Tarpleywick farm by Tarpley's kin.

Concurrently with the close of the Boyd Miller tenancy, John W. Ruby and Laura T. Ruby signed a contract for the sale of Tarpleywick to Albert and Anna Wille of Williamsburg, Iowa County, Iowa.

The Rubys received from the Albert Willes 470 acres of land near Grand Forks, North Dakota, for which they realized a little less than $25,000, and took back a mortgage on Tarpleywick for $30,000. The proceeds of this land sale and the sale of all the livestock and equipment they owned gave John and Laura what was then considered a competence on which to retire. John continued for many years to add to the income from their investments, by building houses for rent or for sale and to otherwise work at the carpenter trade in Des Moines.

Chapter Sixteen

THE WILLE FAMILY ✣ 1917–1928

ALBERT WILLE and his wife Anna had both been born in Germany, and it was not until sometime after their marriage that they migrated to the United States and settled on a farm in Iowa County, Iowa, near Williamsburg. In 1916 when the Willes purchased Tarpleywick, Albert was sixty years old and had retired. He and Anna had a comfortable home in the town of Williamsburg. Their children were grown—the oldest was thirty-four and the youngest eighteen.

Why did Albert Wille want to buy Tarpleywick? Such evidence as is available indicates that he dreamed of having all his children, four sons and one daughter, established in homes in the same neighborhood. His son George told me, "Father purchased the land to keep the family near one another so that he and mother could spend part of their time visiting us and enjoying all their grandchildren." The following record will indicate in what measure this ideal situation was realized.

In the spring of 1917 the Wille's son-in-law, Fred Eichhorst, and his family moved into the Tarpleywick residence. His wife, Anna Wille, was then twenty-five years old. They had two young sons. The Wille's third son, Fred, then twenty-three, moved into the tenant house and farmed part of the Tarpleywick land from 1917 to 1923. He boarded himself until June of 1918 when he married Zola Brown, the oldest daughter of Nat and Eva Brown of the Stockport area. In 1919 or 1920 Albert Wille had a house built across the road west of the Tarpleywick residence. His son, John, then thirty-four, moved into the new house in 1920 and farmed for three years. When he left, the youngest son, George, then twenty-five, moved into the house and farmed until the end of the farming season of 1925.

On November 17, 1925, Albert Wille died and the family experiment ended. After that the house and all the land which had been farmed by John and George was leased to a tenant. The Eichhorsts remained until the end of the farming season of 1926. For the year 1927 all the land was rented. In the meantime Anna Wille, Albert Wille's widow, was negotiating the sale of the land.

Albert Wille and his wife Anna had spent about five months of each year with the Eichhorsts from 1917 until Albert's death. The remainder of the year was spent in their home in Williamsburg.

To sum up the record, as to the extent to which Albert Wille's dream was fulfilled, all the members of his family, except the oldest, Henry, who died in 1918, participated in the undertaking. But only during the years 1921, 1922, and 1923 were there as many as three of his children there at the same time. When he died, there were just two, Anna and George.

The type of farming done by Fred Eichhorst and the Wille brothers was a combination of crop and livestock farming, characteristic of that part of Iowa, with considerable emphasis on broilers and hogs. They plowed much of the sloping land along Rock Creek which had been in pasture, and thus started the land use practices that later led to the impoverishment of the Tarpleywick land.

Each of the Wille families independently farmed a part of the land, although some of the machinery was held in common, and they worked together, especially in haymaking time. Our information is sketchy, but the following quotations will be helpful. Unfortunately, I was unable to get any statements from Fred Eichhorst, but Fred Wille's wife, Zola Brown Wille, now Mrs. Leo Johnson of Stockport, Iowa, wrote me a letter dated December 26, 1966, from which I quote:

Fred Wille and I were married in June, 1918, and moved away from the farm and locality in 1923. . . . We lived in the little house east of Rock Creek. The farms were never operated as one unit, but the men exchanged farm work during haymak-

ing, etc. . . . Livestock, corn and oats were the principal source
of income, although I raised a large, and I mean a *large*, flock
of chickens each year we were there. We raised barley and buck-
wheat also and some sorghum but the other families did not. All
of them had lots of hay.

In a letter from George Wille dated November 27, 1966,
we find a statement indicating that a special emphasis was
put upon pig production:

Eichhorst built the hog house on the Tarpley Taylor place
(must have been about 1921 or 1922). . . . A hog house was built
on the place where Fred Wille lived. Probably built about 1921.
. . . All of us raised corn. Most of it was fed to hogs. A little
was sold. We raised oats and hay. Livestock consisted of cows
and young cattle, sheep, chickens (John had no chickens). We
did not farm together; however, we helped one another. Each
had his own stock. All except John raised chickens; we counted
on this for part of our income. We raised Buff Orpington chickens and sold them for thirty-five cents a pound. They were considered the prize chickens and weighed just under two pounds.
They were fryers.

At that time there was a chicken dealer in Stockport
who gathered up the chickens that farmers were raising for
the market and shipped them by rail to eastern markets. A
letter from Marguerite Beswick dated January 22, 1968, tells
about it. "Most of those chicken cars went to Buffalo and New
York, we were told, one or two per week through most of
the year. It brought a lot of needed cash into Stockport in
those years." This was before the great development of
specialization in the production of fryers or of eggs in large
production units, where fryers are produced by the hundreds
of thousands in one plant, where the chickens' feet never
touch the ground, and where hens are kept in cages with
thousands under one management.

Speaking of the depression of 1921, George Wille writes,
"These were gloomy days. Although there were no fore-
closures (on any of the Wille land) the depression was very
keenly felt and was, as a matter of fact, one of the reasons I
decided to leave. I will also add, that for my wife and me,
the move to Stockport, Iowa, was the poorest move we ever
made."

The depression of 1921 was due to a sudden drop in land
values and a great drop in the prices of farm products. The

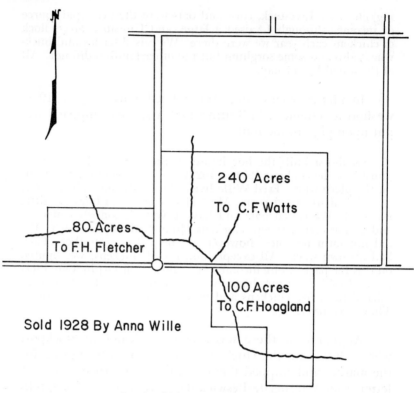

Land sold in 1928 by Anna Wille

average value per acre of land in Van Buren County, Iowa, in 1910 was approximately $80 as shown by the U.S. Census for 1910. In 1920 the average value of land per acre in that county was $135, but in 1930 the census figure was approximately $61. Since Tarpleywick was purchased by the Willes early in 1917, prior to the great land boom of 1919 and 1920, the change in land values did not immediately affect the situation at Tarpleywick. It was the great drop in prices of farm products that made farming unprofitable for George Wille and all other farmers in Iowa who had become used to the wartime prices of farm products. But in the case of farmers who contracted for land at the 1920 prices, the great drop in land values, along with the drop in prices for farm products, threw them into bankruptcy.

By 1928 when Albert Wille's widow, Anna Wille, sold the land, land values were such that she found it necessary to accept appreciably less than she and her husband had paid for the land. The recorded deeds do not show the prices received for the three pieces of land she sold, but it appears from such evidence as is available that the sale of the land, as recorded at the end of February, 1928, yielded more than enough to pay off the mortgage of $30,000 which had been given to the Rubys eleven years earlier.

All the land at Tarpleywick and all three houses were occupied by tenants for the farming year 1927; all the members of the Wille family had entered other occupations. By March 1, 1928, the widow, Anna Wille, had sold in three pieces all the 420 acres the Willes had bought in 1917.

Thus ended the experiment of Albert Wille in assembling his family in one neighborhood group. All members of the family had been involved in the experiment and, having found the plan unsatisfactory from an economic point of view, had moved to other occupations.

The sale of the Tarpleywick land by Anna Wille completed the fragmentation of Tarpleywick which had been started by the Rubys. The 80 acres in section 16, on which the Willes had built a house and on which there was a barn in Tarpley's day, was sold to Floy Harlan Fletcher. The 100 acres in section 22 were bought by C. F. Hoagland. The three eighties in section 15 went to C. F. Watts; thus the land connected with the Tarpleywick headquarters was reduced to 240 acres.

The 80 acres in section 16 was permanently withdrawn from Tarpleywick. The Fletchers held this eighty and farmed it well until December 2, 1957, when they sold it to Paul L. Brown, who was a descendant of an oldtimer in the neighborhood. The 100 acres in section 22 is still held by a member of the Hoagland family.

The unhappy history of the C. F. Watts' investment in Tarpleywick is told in the next chapter.

Chapter Seventeen

TARPLEYWICK IN DISTRESS ❖ 1928–1944

J UST WHY C. F. Watts bought the 240 acres forming the central part of Tarpleywick has not been discovered. He was a physician and surgeon in Williamsburg, Iowa County, where Mrs. Wille was living when she sold Tarpleywick. He had a large farm at Farson where he raised registered Hereford cattle. Farson is in the northeast corner of Wapello County. The distance of this purebred cattle farm from Williamsburg was about thirty-five miles. The distance of Tarpleywick from Williamsburg was about sixty miles. The distance from the cattle farm to Tarpleywick was about thirty miles. All these distances are straight-line measurements from point to point. The highway distances would be greater. It is obvious, therefore, that Dr. Watts' supervision of his farms could not have been very close while he was practicing medicine in Williamsburg. It was also obvious that he was interested in farming, and particularly in purebred cattle.

From 1928 to 1930, Dr. Watts leased the three eighties in section 15 to Lem and Ray Standley. Lem lived in the old Tarpleywick farmhouse on the corner at the center of Cedar Township, and Ray lived in the tenant house east of Rock Creek. In 1930 Dr. Watts brought a herd of his cattle down there and hired Roy Sullivan by the month to look after the cattle, farm the place, and raise some hogs.

Dr. Watts had borrowed a considerable sum from the Equitable Life Assurance Association of New York when he bought Tarpleywick. By the end of 1933 land values in Iowa had sunk to a very low level and the Equitable Life

Assurance Association started foreclosure on a very large number of Iowa farms, including that part of Tarpleywick held by Dr. Watts.

In the spring of 1934 Dr. Watts moved the cattle back to Farson. When he moved his cattle from Tarpleywick he had obviously decided not to contest the foreclosure. He leased the land to a share-tenant for the remainder of his period of possession, and the Equitable was granted title to the land on December 2, 1935, by the Van Buren County Court.

The Equitable leased the land to Floyd Rehkopf who was at that time occupying the Tarpleywick farmhouse. Rehkopf paid a share of the crop and cash rent for the pastureland. He remained until 1942, when Jim Stillwell moved on. C. A. Warner bought the land from the Equitable on February 2, 1943, but let Jim Stillwell stay on until March 1944.

To summarize the management of Tarpleywick from 1928 to 1943 under the ownership of C. F. Watts and the Equitable, I quote from a letter dated January 10, 1967, from Floy Harlan Fletcher, who had moved onto the eighty in section 16 in 1928 and lived in the house built by the Willes. She was a close observer of what was happening on this central remnant of Tarpleywick:

When we moved on the eighty we purchased in 1928, Lem Standley lived on the corner and Ray Standley lived in the house down east of Rock Creek. They lived there until 1930 when C. F. Watts brought a herd of his cattle down there and hired Roy Sullivan by the month to look after the cattle and farm the place and raise some hogs until the spring of 1934 when he moved the cattle back to Farson and John Hoffer moved into the east house and paid grain rent for two years and moved off. In 1934 Floyd Rehkopf moved into the house on the corner. When John Hoffer moved off (1935), Rehkopf took all the place over until the spring of 1942 when he had a sale and moved to Ottumwa. In March 1942 Jim Stillwell moved on and paid grain rent for field crops and cash rent for meadows and pastures and buildings.

The management of Tarpleywick during this period when it was operated by tenants had taken its toll. As a rule, the tenants had given primary attention to the production of corn and oats and minimum attention to hay and pasture. To extend the cropland they plowed up the meadows and pastures. This management of the land resulted in depletion of the soil. In addition to the soil depletion by heavy cropping, erosion had taken even a heavier toll. Furthermore, the buildings and fences had been allowed to deteriorate.

I visited Tarpleywick in 1936 and was shocked. Its run-down condition distressed me greatly and I considered buying the 240 acres with a view to its restoration. I had it appraised by two separate appraisers. One appraised it at $35 per acre and the other at $40. I decided that I might pay $50 an acre. I was living in Chicago at that time and could have visited the farm for a few days at least once a month, and for sentimental reasons thought I would like to own it. I wrote to the Equitable in New York, asking what they would take for the land. The man who was in charge of land sales was an acquaintance of mine and to my surprise asked $100 an acre. As this was more than twice the appraised value, I declined the offer. Thereupon the Equitable's agent offered the land to me for $50 an acre, but in the meantime I had bought land near Madison, Wisconsin. Seven years later C. A. Warner bought Tarpleywick.

Chapter Eighteen

THE WARNERS

THE CENTRAL PART of Tarpleywick was deeded to Charles Augustus Warner and his wife by the Equitable Life Assurance Association of the United States on February 2, 1943.

C. A. Warner, as he signs letters and documents, is known in the neighborhood as "Gus." He and his wife Ethel Ada, have a family of five children, two sons and three daughters. At the time they bought Tarpleywick they were farming near Batavia, about twenty-one miles northwest of Stockport. The Warner's lease on the Batavia farm did not end until March 1, 1944, so Jim Stillwell continued to farm Tarpleywick for another year.

On March 1, 1944, the Warners moved to Tarpleywick. Gus and Ethel moved into the Tarpleywick residence and their second son Jim and his wife moved into the tenant house a quarter-mile east. Their first task was to establish a system of farming that would rebuild the productivity of the land. The first year they planted a large acreage of oats as a nurse crop for seeding down much of the land into permanent pasture. They also used various other methods to stop the erosion which had been destroying the farm. The buildings and fences needed repair, and the Tarpleywick residence was so dilapidated that they tore it down and built a new house.

On June 1, 1966, when I visited the Warners, they were farming not only the 240 acres in section 15 but were also leasing an additional 100 acres in section 22. That year all the land in the southwest quarter of section 15 was in pasture

The new Tarpleywick house

Gang of four mouldboard plows drawn by a tractor of the kind in use by the Warners.

First Farmall tractor (Courtesy International Harvester Company)

Farmall tractor cultivating corn

or meadow, except for 10 acres of corn and 6 acres of oats. In 1965 they had planted 60 acres of corn and the yield had been more than 100 bushels per acre. They had used Pioneer hybrid seed corn and considerable commercial fertilizer. The oat crop was limited to 28 acres. Forty acres of meadow were cut for hay; 15 acres of this were alfalfa and 25 acres were mixed clover and timothy. To summarize the land usage, 128 acres were in temporary meadow, oats, and corn; buildings, barnyards, and gardens occupied about 10 acres; this left about 200 acres in permanent pasture.

The crop rotation, corn, oats, and hay, was the same my father had used, but the machinery had changed greatly since his day. He had kept twenty to twenty-five horses, but the Warners had disposed of their last horse in 1950. They had three all-purpose tractors, one that would draw a four-bottom plow, one that would draw three, and one that would draw two. The smallest tractor was used mainly for pulling the trailers that have taken the place of wagons. All the farm equipment that had been drawn by horses in the old days was drawn by tractors.

The development of a tractor which could be used for the cultivation of corn was a major step in eliminating the need for horses on the farm. In 1924 the first Farmall tractor was built with the front wheels placed very close together. The rear wheels of the tractor straddled two rows of corn while the close-together front wheels ran between these rows. It pushed a two-row cultivator. The problem of cultivating corn without horses was solved.

At Tarpleywick in 1965 corn was planted by a four-row

Four-row corn planter with fertilizer and herbicide equipment drawn by tractor.

Small tractor-drawn combine harvester and thresher put on the market by Allis-Chalmers in the middle 1930s.

Self-propelled twelve-foot cut combine used at Tarpleywick.

corn planter that carried auxiliary boxes for fertilizer and
herbicides. It was cultivated not more than twice with a four-
row corn cultivator, and finally it was harvested by a two-row
cornhusker that delivered the ears of corn to a trailer.

After the corn had been picked, the cattle were turned
into the field to clean up any corn left behind and the forage
found along the turning rows. This had been my father's
practice. In preparing land for seeding oats, it was kept in
mind that oat land would be in meadow the following year.
Along with the oats a mixture of clover and timothy or
alfalfa was seeded. The land was prepared by using a disc
harrow and a spike-toothed harrow. The seed was planted
with a drill having a box for oats and another for grass seed.
An itinerant combine with a twelve-foot cut harvested the
oats.

The fifteen acres of alfalfa were cut three times. The
first cutting of clover and timothy mixture was used for hay

Hay-cutting and conditioning machine drawn by tractor. Greatly reduces time required for curing hay in the swatch and reduces shattering of the leaves.

Tractor-drawn hay-baler taking cured hay from the swatch.

Spotted Poland China and Duroc Jersey cross-bred hogs raised by the Warners.

and the second growth of clover was either cut for seed or for hay. The hay was cut and conditioned by a machine with double rollers that flattened the stems so that the stems cured as quickly as the leaves. It was cured in the swath and when dry enough was picked up by a baler that pushed the bales back onto a trailer which carried them to the barn where they were put into the mow, either by an elevator or by a hayfork of a kind formerly used for loose hay.

Livestock of the farm included cross-bred hogs, Black Angus cattle, and Corriedale sheep. The hogs produced the largest part of the gross income. They were cross-bred hogs produced by using a spotted Poland-China boar one year and a Duroc Jersey boar the next. The average litter was eight, and there were two litters per year. He used his brood sows for two years and then sent them to market, so that each year half of this thirty-six brood sows would be gilts. In 1966 he produced more than 500 pigs for market. They yielded the largest total income from pigs he had ever realized, even though the prices were not as high as they were in 1965.

Once the pigs are weaned and the sows rebred, the handling of the pigs becomes almost automatic as far as the feeding is concerned. At this point what Mr. Warner called "the corn bank" takes a hand. The "corn bank" is a corn storage service run by the Prairie Grain Company, a $300,000 corporation in Stockport. It will send a corn sheller to the farm, truck the shelled corn to the elevator, test it for moisture, dry it if necessary, and store it. As it is needed on the farm, enough corn to refill the automatic feeders is ground and mixed with high-protein concentrate and such antibiotics or worm medicine as may be specified. Purina was mentioned by C. A. Warner as the concentrate being used when we were there in 1966. The feed mixture is then delivered and put into the self-feeders. All of this service costs the farmer about $1 per 220-pound hog, finished. The "corn bank" has 150 or more customers like Warner.

In a letter from Raymond Keller, manager of the Prairie Grain Company, dated December 26, 1968, he states:

As to the shelling of the corn we charge 3 cents per bushel and 1 cent per bushel for a crew we furnish to scoop or move the corn into the sheller. Also, we charge 3 cents per bushel for hauling corn to the elevator with our trucks. Then if the corn

Corn silos at the "corn bank" in Stockport, Iowa, three miles west of Tarpleywick.

is over 15.5 percent moisture we have a drying charge. This is a charge of a minimum of 5 cents per bushel and ½ cent per point of moisture removed over 5 percent. . . . The drying charge is 5 cents per bushel for the first 5 percent of moisture removed.

Incidentally, this grain dryer will dry 36,000 bushels of corn a day, removing 10 percent of extra moisture to make the corn storable. It burns a maximum of 3,600 gallons of propane gas a day.

Getting back to the feeding operation, we then take this 15.5 percent dryer corn and mix it with Purina Commercial feed concentrate. We charge 15 cents a hundred for grinding and $1 per ton delivery on the mixed feed, usually making for a total of about $1 per head total expense for the farmer per 220-pound hog finished.

We shipped this last year about 980 carloads of corn and soybeans and shipped in about 80 carloads of fertilizer for feed. Much of our feed and fertilizer, though, probably about 66 percent, comes in by truck.

This corn we ship goes to various destinations: St. Louis; Kansas City; Atchison, Kansas; Keokuk, Iowa; and of course for export. The soybeans go to soybean processors. We ship by truck to barge loading points, probably about 800,000 bushels of corn and soybeans annually. This is loaded on barges and goes down the Mississippi River for export overseas. It is unloaded at the gulf and loaded on ocean liners.

As to the number of people we deliver feed to, I would guess approximately 150 or more regular customers.

Next in importance to the hogs is the herd of Black Angus. In 1966 there were sixty-six brood cows, two-thirds of which were registered. The calves were sold off the cows at weaning time, except for ten or twelve heifers every year, which were kept for replenishing the herd. A few purebred bulls were sold for breeding purposes. Calves sold in the fall weigh 500 pounds, and big calves bring $125 each. They were sold at from twenty-three to thirty-five cents a pound to a man who runs an auction barn. On May 15, 1966, he sold early calves at thirty cents a pound. In a letter dated April 29, 1967, C. A. Warner wrote, "We have ninety-six brood cows."

In 1965 the Warners had a hundred Corriedale ewes, in 1966 they had ninety. They were planning to reduce their

The Warners of Tarpleywick in 1967. Ethel and Gus pause to sit on the front lawn of their home.

flock to sixty ewes. There are many twin lambs so the lamb crop sometimes runs as high as 150 percent. Lambs sold in late May or early June weighed about ninety pounds on the average, and brought from $18 to $25 a head.

A yearling lamb may shear as high as twenty-six pounds. This is the top. It appears that hogs and cattle are the larger sources of income.

Hogs, cattle, and sheep provide the income from the 340 acres of the old Tarpleywick farm now operated by Gus and Jim Warner. The gross income for the year 1965 was $21,558.17. This is about ten times as large a gross income as my father received in 1893 when he was farming 510 acres. Gus Warner is receiving prices for cattle, hogs, and sheep about ten times as high as Tarpley was receiving in the nineties, but the dollar in 1893 would purchase ten times as much as in 1965. Tarpley was able to send two of his children to college in 1893. This would have cost at least $5,000 in 1965. It cost less than $500 in 1893.

Gus Warner has restored Tarpleywick to its former prosperity. As long as the farm was owned by the Rubys I was a frequent visitor. After the Rubys sold the farm I did not see it again until 1936. When I drove into the yard at that time, a red Farmall tractor was standing outside the kitchen door. After I had talked to the tenant farmer and had seen the sorry state of the buildings and the land, that red tractor seemed to symbolize his attitude toward the farm. He was interested only in exploiting the land for short-term cash return. It had made me heartsick to see my father's farm in such distress and it took me thirty years to gather courage to take another look. When we drove into the yard in 1966, everything was in order. A freshly painted modern house stood where the old Tarpleywick house had stood; the lawn was well kept; the buildings were in repair. It is a pleasure to know that Tarpleywick is in such good hands. The changes in farming during the century considered in this book are certainly dramatic, but there is also a constant factor that remains unchanged—the attitude of the good farmer toward his land.

INDEX

Animals. *See* Livestock *and* Wildlife
Apple butter, making of, 36–37
Appleby knotter, 83–84

Barns, 63–64
Barnyard, 28, 29
Baumann, George, 103
Beekeeping, 14, 42–43
Big Cedar Creek, crossing, 77
Birds, 25–26
Blacksmith shop, 4
Blundy, Elda, 21
Bonapart (town), 77, 79
Brown, Eva, 113
Brown, Nat, 113
Brown, Paul L., 117
Brush, 23
Buildings, 27–33
Butchering, hog, 37–39

Campbell, Bert, 103
Cattle, 72–73, 110, 129
  in 1850, 7
  in 1870, 18
  in 1880, 20–21
  See also Sheds
Cedar Township, 4
Cellar, 45–46
Census Schedules
  for 1850, 7
  for 1860, 8
  for 1870, 18–19
  for 1880, 20–21
Chickens. *See* Poultry
Clark, Frank, 88
Clover, 49, 50
Coal bank, 21, 27
Cooking, 7

Corn, 6, 16, 49, 50
  bank, 127–129
  cultivating, 85
  in 1860, 8
  in 1870, 18
  in 1880, 21
  husking, 52, 70–71
  meal, 14
  stalk cutter, 61
  See also Seeding
Cradle, 16
Cropland, 19
Crops, 111
  production in 1850, 7
  production in 1870, 18–19
  See also Clover, Corn, Flax, Hay,
    Land usage, Oats, Rotation,
    Timothy, *and* Wheat
Cropper, 26, 88–89
Cultivation, 14–16, 51, 53–61
  corn, 57–59, 85
Cultivator, 58–59

Depression of 1921, 115–116
Dinner bell, 28, 42
Disc, 61
Doctoring. *See* Medicine, folk
Dogs, 24
Drainage, 26. *See also* Erosion
Drake University, 75, 99, 104
Drying of fruits and vegetables,
  46–47

Economy of Tarpleywick, 47. *See
  also* Self-sufficiency
Education. *See* Schools *and* Training
Eichhorst, Fred, 113
Ely, Richard T. (professor), 100

Equitable Life Insurance Association, as mortgage holder, 118–120
Equipment. *See* Implements
Erosion, 26, 119–120
Expansion of Tarpleywick, 18–22, 92. *See also* Land, acquisition

Fair, Grange, 97–98
Fairfield (town), 77, 79
Fences, 20, 33–35
Fertilizer, 20, 52
Fields, 23–26
Flax (1880), 21
Fletcher, Floy Harlan, 117, 119
Food, 13–14, 45–47, 107–108
  storage, 45–46
  See also Butchering, Gardens, Orchards, Salting, Sausage making, *and* Smoking
Fort Madison (town), 16–17, 76
Fruits, 13–14
  apples, in 1880, 21
  See also Drying, Food, Orchards, *and* Peaches
Fry (Tarpley's cousin), 87

Gardens, 44–45, 81
Geese. *See* Poultry
Grading, uniform, need for, 87
Granary, "ever-normal," 29–30
Grange, 96–98

Harlan, Edgar, 98–99
Harlan family, 9–10
Harrow, 53–54, 60, 125
Harvest, 16, 62–71
Hastings, Louella. *See* Taylor, Anna Louella
Hay, 8, 16, 125–127
  fork, 32
  loader, 64
  rack, 63
  rake, 62, 63
Hazel brush, 23, 24
Heating
  of house, 7
  of school, 10
Hillsboro (town), 76
Hoaglund, C. F., 117
Hogs, 31–32, 71, 73–74, 127
  in 1850, 7
  in 1870, 18
  in 1880, 21
  marketing, 77–78
Homestead Act, 18, 92
Honey. *See* Beekeeping

Horse barn, 29
Horses, 8, 72, 124
  in 1850, 7
  in 1870, 18
  in 1880, 20
  See also Implements
Houses, 4, 6, 7, 12, 16, 121
  tenant, 27
Hunting
  rabbit, 23–24
  squirrel, 25
Husking peg, 16

Implements, farm, 16, 32–33, 53–61, 62–71, 81–85, 123–125
  value of, in 1870, 18; in 1880, 20
Income, 75, 130. *See also* Census Schedules
Infares. *See* Weddings
Iowa State College, 75, 99

Johnson, Mrs. Leo. *See* Wille, Zola Brown

Keosauqua (town), 77

Labor, 20
  scheduling, 50–52, 84, 85, 88
  wages paid (1870), 18; (1879), 20
  See also Women, work of
Land
  acquisition, early Taylor family, 4, 6, 8; Tarpleywick, 11, 17, 19, 21
  sold, 8
  usage, 20, 48–52, 123
Lazenby, John, 88
Livestock, 6, 7, 8–9, 72–76, 110–111, 127
  in 1870, 18–19
  in 1880, 20
  marketing, 77–78
  value of animals slaughtered, 9
Lockridge (town), 76–77
Loom, 9
Lumber, 7, 16

Machinery. *See* Implements
McVeigh (town), 78–79
Manure hauling, 52
Marketing, 111
Markets, 76–79
Martin, Alexander (grandfather), 9, 21, 48, 103

Martin, Anna Harlan (grandmother), 9
Martin, Elmira. *See* Taylor, Elmira Martin
Martin, George (brother of Elmira), 12
Meadow. *See* Clover *and* Timothy
Meat. *See* Butchering, Livestock, Salting, Sausage making, *and* Smoking
Medicine, folk, 13, 102
Milk production. *See* Cattle
Miller, Boyd, 112
Miller, Alta Wheatly, 112
Mills, 77
  corn, grinding, 33
  fanning, 32
  saw and planing, 16
Molasses. *See* Sorghum
Morris, Carrie. *See* Taylor, Carrie Morris
Morris, Henry, 9
Morris, Henry T. (son), 9
Morris, Jane (Mrs. Henry), 9
Mortgage. *See* Equitable Life Insurance Association
Mower, 63. *See also* Reaper
Mules, 8, 72
  in 1850, 7
  in 1870, 18

Nuts, 24

Oats, 49, 50
  in 1870, 18
  in 1880, 21
  as nurse crop, 60
  seeding, 125
Orchards, 13–14, 45
  products, value of, in 1880, 21
Oxen, 6, 8
  in 1850, 7
  See also Cattle

Peaches, packed for market, 87
Planter, corn, 124–125
Planting. *See* Seeding
Plowing, 6, 50–51
Plows, 14
  mouldboard, 53
Population, of Iowa, 1840 and 1860, 4
Potatoes
  in 1870, 18
  in 1880, 21
Poultry, 75, 115
  in 1880, 21
Prairie land, broken, 9

Production. *See* Crop production, Livestock, *and* Self-sufficiency
Profits. *See* Income
Pumps, 27–28

Railroads, 76–77, 78
Rake. *See* Hay rake
Reaper, 65–68, 81–84
Rehkopf, Floyd, 119
Religion, 94–96
Roads, Cedar Township, 4
Rock Creek, 23
  influence on drainage, 26
Rocky, Jake, 73, 95
Roller, 61
Rotation, crop, 49–52, 123. *See also* Land usage
Ruby, Boyd, 109–111
Ruby, Gladys Carolyn, 107–108, 111
Ruby, Helen Elmira, 111
Ruby, Jabez, 19
Ruby, John, 40–41, 107–112
Ruby, Laura. *See* Taylor, Ruby
Ruby, Laura Kathryn (daughter), 111
Ruby, Taylor, 109–111

Salting meat, 39
Sausage making, 38
Schools, 10–11, 87, 98–100
Scott (professor), 100
Scythe, 16, 62, 64–65
Seeding, 50–51, 53–61
  clover, 60
  corn, 54–57
  oats, 59–60
  timothy, 60
Self-sufficiency of Tarpleywick, 14, 45–47, 107–108, 111
Sheds for cattle and sheep, 30–31
Sheep, 8–9, 74, 129–130
  in 1850, 7
  in 1870, 18
  in 1880, 21
  used in cultivating, 51
  See also Sheds
Sheller, corn, 32–33
Shivarees. *See* Weddings
Shocks, 65
Sigler, Meshak, 16
Size of farm, 18–19
  comparisons, 22
  in 1850, 7
  See also Land, acquisition
Slaughtering. *See* Butchering
Smokehouse, 28–29
Smoking meat, 39
Soap, laundry, making, 41–42

Sorghum, 14, 21
Spinning, 9, 13
Standley family, 4
Standley, Lem, 118
Standley, Ray, 118
Steamboat, 86
Stillwell, Jim, 119
Stockport (town), 79
Sullivan, Roy, 118
Swine. *See* Hogs

Tarpley, Mary. *See* Taylor, Mary
    Tarpley
Tarpley, William, 3
Taylor, Anna (cousin), 102–103
Taylor, Anna Louella (Lou), 98,
    101, 104, 108–109
Taylor, Carrie (sister), 40, 103–104,
    107, 108–109
Taylor, Carrie Morris, (Mrs. Syl-
    vanus), 98
Taylor, Charlie (uncle), 6, 13
Taylor, Eliza Walker (Mrs. Wil-
    liam), 5–6
Taylor, Elizabeth (Mrs. George
    Baumann), 102–103
Taylor, Elmira Martin (Mrs. Tarp-
    ley), 9, 11, 12–17, 42, 44, 101–106
Taylor, George (cousin), 102–103
Taylor, John Pleasant, 102
Taylor, Laura (Mrs. John Ruby),
    56, 98, 107–112
Taylor, Lou. *See* Taylor, Anna
    Louella
Taylor, Mary Tarpley (Mrs.
    George), 3
Taylor, Mary Zumwalt, 4
Taylor, Richard, 3
Taylor, Sylvanus (brother), 16, 23–
    24, 28, 40–41, 98, 111
Taylor, Tarpley (great-great-grand-
    father), 3
Taylor, Tarpley Early (father), 3,
    10–11, 12–17, 19–20, 29–30, 31,
    34, 42, 44–45, 46, 50, 52, 53, 62,
    64, 65, 73, 77–78, 80–89, 90–100,
    106
Taylor, William Allen (uncle), 109
Taylor, William Early (grand-
    father), 3, 4–6, 10, 11, 19, 63
Taylor, William (cousin), 102–103
Teachers, 10
Tenants. *See* Croppers
Threshing, 51, 68–70, 111
Threshing machine, 16
    engine of, used in sawing wood,
    40–41
Timberland, 6–7, 16, 23–26. *See*
    also Trees *and* Wood
Timothy, 49
Township, 3–4

Tractors, 123–124
Training
    of a farmer, 80–89
    See also Schools
Transportation, 13, 17
Travel, 86
Trees, 23. *See also* Timberland
    and Wood
Turkey. *See* Poultry
Turnpike at Louisiana, Missouri, 11

Vacation to Louisiana, Missouri,
    85–87
Value of farm
    in 1850, 7
    in 1870, 18–19
    in 1880, 20–21
    See also Income
Vegetables. *See* Drying, Food, *and*
    Gardens

Walker, Eliza. *See* Taylor, Eliza
    Walker
Walker family, 5
Warner, Charles Augustus (Gus),
    119, 121
Warner, Ethel Ada, 121
Warner, Jim (son), 121
Water, 27–28
    holes, 23
    See also Wells
Watson, Elmer, 89
Watts, C. F., 117, 118–119
Weaving, 28–29
Weddings, 104
Wells, 27–28. *See also* Water
Wheat, 6, 8, 14
    in 1870, 18
    in 1880, 21
Wildlife, 25
Wille, Albert, 112, 113–117
Wille, Anna (Mrs. Fred Eichhorst),
    112, 113–117
Wille, Fred, 113
Wille, George, 113, 114, 115
Wille, Henry, 114
Wille, John, 113, 114
Wille, Zola Brown, 113, 114–115
Wilsonville (town), 76
Windmill, 27
Women, work of, 12–13
Wood
    cutting, 80–81
    supply, 39–41
    yard, 36–43
    See also Timberland *and* Trees
Work. *See* Labor

Zumwalt family, 11